✦ DISTILLED IN ✦
BOSTON

A HISTORY & GUIDE WITH COCKTAIL RECIPES

ZACHARY LAMOTHE

AMERICAN PALATE

Published by American Palate
A Division of The History Press
Charleston, SC
www.historypress.com

Front cover, top left: photo by Reagan Byrne; *top center*: photo by Holbrooke Garcia; *top right*: photo by author; *bottom*: courtesy of Bully Boy Distillers. *Back cover*: photo by Kendra Dott's Double Exposure; *insert*: courtesy of Adirondack Barrel Cooperage.

First published 2023

Manufactured in the United States

ISBN 9781467151214

Library of Congress Control Number: 2023932114

Notice: The information in this book is true and complete to the best of our knowledge. It is offered without guarantee on the part of the author or The History Press. The author and The History Press disclaim all liability in connection with the use of this book.

This one is for Charlie.

Contents

Contents

ACKNOWLEDGEMENTS

F irst and foremost, another tremendous thank-you to my wife, Jackie, and my three boys, Danny, Tommy and Charlie. From never batting an eye when I had to do my "field research" (drinking), to coming with me to certain distilleries, my appreciation for you is endless. Thanks also to my mom and dad, who have always been the utmost champions of my writing, and an extra thanks to my mom, the forever editor of my work.

A big thanks to my editor, Mike Kinsella. Without him, this project would not have been possible. A very special thanks to Rhonda Kallman, who, along with Mike, were involved in this project before even I was. A huge shout-out to friends and family who joined me in one aspect or another of the research: Jim Wheeler, James Hutchinson, Collin Ward, Adam Mannar (thanks for the ride, guys), Dave Lehan, Dave Halperin, Zack, Laura, Annabelle and Samantha Lee and, of course, Jackie.

A tip of the cap goes to the following individuals, who welcomed me with open arms and bottle in hand to their amazing distilleries: Andrew McCabe at AstraLuna Brands; Rhonda Kallman and John Stark at Boston Harbor Distillery; Will Willis at Bully Boy Distillers; John Sorgini, Kyle Leclerc, Sylvan Peter and Kassandra Laskarides at Chattermark Distillers; Jesse Brenneman at Deacon Giles Distillery; Brenton MacKechnie at Dirty Water Distillery; Patrick and Beth Downing at GlenPharmer Distillery; Matt Nuernberger at GrandTen Distilling; Justin Pelletier at Nashoba Valley Spirits; Andrew Cabot at Privateer Rum; Bob Ryan at Ryan & Wood Distilleries; Zachary

Robinson at Short Path Distillers; Beth Crowell at South Hollow Spirits; and John and Kelly Lendall at Working Man Distillers. An additional thank-you to the distilleries that provided many of the photos used in this book.

Thanks to Mary Ann Buckley for introducing me to the *Mr. Boston Guide*, and to Jonathan Pogash, Irene Tan and Kelly Blazosky for their unique stories.

INTRODUCTION

Welcome to the wonderful world of craft distilleries in the Boston area. From the North Shore to the South Shore, from the Cape to Nantucket, and of course in Beantown itself, let this book guide you through the region's excellent selection of craft distilleries, each with its own backstory and each with a distinct repertoire of fantastic spirits to sample along the way. Dive into the region's distilling history. Did you know that once upon a time Boston and the coastal towns to the north of it were a hotbed for rum manufacturing?

Craft distilling in the region during the modern era began in 2000, with the opening of Triple Eight Distillery on Nantucket. With new distilleries springing up every year, by the time this book is in print, there will certainly be others to visit. From bourbon to rum, vodka to gin, whatever your libation of choice is, there is a Boston-area distillery for you. Some, such as Boston Harbor Distillery and Privateer Rum, are rooted in regional history, while others, including GrandTen and Short Path, have an uber-cool speakeasy vibe. Some, such as Nashoba Valley Spirits, are located on farms; others, including Bully Boy, are in the middle of the city. Some are in vacation destinations, including Triple Eight, South Hollow Spirits in Truro and AstraLuna Brands' Cape and Islands Distillers, which is located in Mashpee. Deacon Giles has a foreboding tale that is perfect for its Salem location, and others, including Ryan & Wood and Privateer, have maritime associations. Some distilleries' products can be found in stores, whereas others are available only at the distillery. Some distillers have been in the industry for decades;

others recently joined the fray. We will also meet individuals who add their own touch to the regional craft scene without actually distilling, including Jonathan Pogash and Irene Tan. Learn where distillers get their ingredients, why they started their business and what makes them love their work.

Meet the owners and distillers who make this region's spirits spectacular. Along with a history of distilling in the region, an overview of distilling and a feature of each distillery, this book also showcases recipes from many of the distilleries so that readers can make their own cocktails at home.

Cheers!

Part I

Distilling in Boston
through the Years

Before we dive into the current era, it is important to reflect on the history of distilling in the Boston area, from the colonial era to the present. Through much of the latter half of the twentieth century, the region was not a hotbed for spirits, but historically, alcohol, namely rum, was an integral part of the economy of the Boston area.

Although the current trend of distilleries in the Boston area is relatively new, starting with Nantucket's Triple Eight Distillery in 2000, the presence of distilleries and distilled spirits in general has become part of the fabric of the region. Boston and its coastal environs played a major role in the notorious triangular trade, in which the importation and exportation of molasses and rum was supplemented by the slave trade. Many Boston-area distilleries manufacture vodka and even whiskey, but historically, rum is the liquor most associated with the Bay State. The roots of rum hearken back to the 1600s, when it was invented in the West Indies. A few decades later, rum manufacture thrived in Boston, and the city boasted numerous distilleries. Even prior to 1690, rum had become associated with Boston. North of the city, distilleries such as Caldwell's in Newburyport and Lawrence Distilling in Medford were some of the most well known in the region. Many of the rum distilleries were located on the shore, where the same proprietors were ship owners as well. Both of these industries were important in colonial America. A perfect example of this was the Cabots, who owned their namesake wharf in Beverly and distilled rum on-site, eventually selling the distillery and wharf to try their hand (successfully) at

A look into the still at AstraLuna Brands. *Photo by author.*

privateering. Today, this legacy lives on in Andrew Cabot's Privateer Rum in Ipswich.

Massachusetts Bay Colony was founded by Puritans, who are often thought of as having an "all work, no play" mentality. In actuality, alcoholic drink is one vice that the Puritans allowed themselves. Rum played a major role in the American colonies and was known especially in the area north of Boston. It was first made in Barbados in the 1640s. Originally, the spirit went by the name *kill devil* for the burning taste; another early term for it was *rumbullion*, which translates as "big quarrel" and thus was shortened to simply *rum*. By 1660, the term *rum* appeared. Unlike other spirits, which can be made from a variety of ingredients, such as whiskey, which can be made from a variety of grains, rum is based on only sugarcane. Some are made from sugarcane juice and some from molasses, but the original ingredient is still sugarcane. Molasses, made from the sugarcane juice of the West Indies, was imported into the New England colonies. Here it was turned into rum, which was traded to Europe and West Africa. In West Africa, an unfortunate return was enslaved persons shipped to the West Indies, supplementing the triangular trade. In the mid-eighteenth century, 25 rum distilleries dotted the landscape in towns such as Watertown, Haverhill and Charlestown, and by 1783, there were 60 rum distilleries in Massachusetts alone. More proof that rum was king was the fact that in 1791, more than seven million gallons of molasses were imported into the state of Massachusetts alone! During the colonial era in New England, there were some 159 distilleries, with rum being the primary product. Rum was used as a celebratory drink for such events as commemorating new construction and social gatherings.

An example of the trade in action would be a ship leaving Boston loaded with barrels of rum. Of course, the crew would imbibe along the route. On reaching Africa, the remaining rum was traded. The ship was then filled with Africans and gold. The ship then traveled to the islands of the West Indies, where the enslaved persons were unloaded to work at the sugarcane plantations. Sent from the West Indies to Boston would be copious hogsheads of molasses. A hogshead is a unit of measure—a cask with about twice the volume as a regular-sized barrel. In Boston, the molasses was used to make rum. Even in the late nineteenth century, when rum manufacture was on the decline, New England was still the place for rum, accounting for seven of the eight rum distilleries nationwide. Massachusetts was the focal point, with six of the seven located in the Bay State.

Although distilleries operated at a steady pace throughout the colonial period, the first stills were not commercial enterprises. These were placed in homes, with the drink used as medicine and as an offering to thirsty guests. Rum was even served at the inauguration of George Washington.

In the towns north of Boston, rum distilling was a popular enterprise. Just north of Boston, the city of Medford was synonymous with its rums, which were available at lower prices. Medford rum distilleries included the names

Left: An Old Fashioned made with Privateer Rum. *Photo by Reagan Byrne.*

Right: Try the White Hot cocktail at Chattermark Distillers. *Photo by Kassandra Laskarides.*

of Bishop, Hall and Blanchard. Hall's distillery began in the early eighteenth century and was passed from John to his brother and then to his son. Daniel Lawrence, who worked at Hall's distillery, eventually acquired the facility and changed its name to Lawrence. Lawrence Distilling was the most popular in Medford. It was founded in 1830 and stayed in business until 1905. Most of the region's distilleries shuttered in the early 1800s for reasons including the Embargo Act and Americans' newfound taste for whiskey. The distillery was located on Ship Street, today called Riverside Avenue. Its Medford Rum was considered by many to be the best in the country, although some scholars question whether it actually tasted good. As an homage to Medford's place in the region's rum history, modern Boston distillery GrandTen distills a Medford Rum. This is a traditional New England rum made in an Old-World way, using blackstrap molasses and wild New England yeast.

Other famous distilleries included Caldwell's Distillery in Newburyport, founded in 1790; John M. Barnard and Company; and one of the most well-known even in the modern era, Mr. Boston. The Mr. Boston distillery, originally known as Old Mr. Boston, was located in Roxbury. Its original tenure lasted from 1933 to 1986. It distilled such spirits as rum, bourbon, brandy and gin. Defunct in 1986, the brand was reestablished by Barton

Brands in 1995. Fourteen years later, in 2009, Sazerac bought Mr. Boston. Sazerac makes a wide variety of liquor under numerous names, including Fireball, Dr. McGillicuddy's and 99 Bananas. Sazerac operates distilleries throughout the United States and abroad but does not operate a distillery in Boston, even though the "Boston" moniker is still used. In addition to the actual liquor, Mr. Boston is also known for the handy reference guide for bartenders that uses its name, which we will be learning more about later.

Caldwell's Distillery in Newburyport was known for its rum. Founded by Alexander Caldwell, it operated for 171 years, not including the years of Prohibition. Like much of the North Shore, especially with access to the harbor, Newburyport was a rum capital, home to numerous distilleries of the spirit. After Prohibition, the Caldwell operation continued, with its final shuttering in 1961. In addition to Newburyport, Boston and Medford, the coastal North Shore towns of Ipswich and Salem were also known for their rum manufacture.

Rum lost its footing in New England for multiple reasons, one of which was its association with slavery. The concept of slavery was anathema to devout Christians in New England. There was also an excise tax placed on the importation of molasses. To combat this, Congress incentivized using products grown in America instead of importing them from foreign lands. The era of rum as king would end by the early years of the 1800s for three primary reasons. The first was the Embargo Act of 1807, which outlawed the importation of cheap British molasses. Second, the legal importation of enslaved persons ceased a year later as the frontier expanded and Americans pushed west. Finally, ingredients needed for whiskey making were found readily and cheaply. Thus whiskey overthrew rum as America's favorite spirit.

Although rum lost its championship status as the most consumed spirit in the country long before Prohibition, by the post-Prohibition years of the mid-1930s, it was still the third most widely produced spirit in the United States. In 1937, four years after the repeal of Prohibition, there were four rum distilleries in Massachusetts, as well as distilleries in four other states. The American rum distillation process, especially that of New England, differs from that of the Caribbean. Its final product is typically much less sweet than that of Caribbean rum.

With rum, there is a wide variety of tastes. Some of the variables include whether it is aged or if additives are used. The aging process enhances the flavor of the spirit and lets it take on the qualities of the oak barrels in which it is stored. Some New England rum was aged in bond. This means that it was made during a single year by one distillery and is one spirit, meaning it is not blended with any others. It also needs to be aged in a barrel for at least four years after distilling and has to be at least 100 proof when it is ready for bottling.

Prior to Prohibition, in the year 1917, three million barrels of rum were produced in Massachusetts alone. This was known as Everett Rum, as distilleries such as the Everett Distilling Company were producing at this time. Rum is produced once again in Everett today, as Short Path Distillery is located in the town just north of Boston. Even after Prohibition, there was New England rum that was aged from before 1920. This was often used for flavoring rum or blending it with other rum. A modern version of a Boston-based rum that is blended with other rum is the Rum Cooperative series from Bully Boy Distillers. They blend their own rum with that of rum from other countries, including Panama, the Dominican Republic and Trinidad, which are the countries featured in their "Volume 1" of the Rum Cooperative series. Distilling rum in the classic New England manner is Privateer, which even ages some of its rum in bond. New England rum was considered a full-bodied rum compared to the lighter and sweeter rums of the Caribbean.

Clearly, alcohol was ingrained in the colonial and post–Revolutionary War society of Massachusetts. In the early to mid-nineteenth century, reform movements swept the young nation, calling for progressive ideals such as an end to slavery and the advocation of women's rights. Alcoholism reached a high point in early 1800s America. In response was a temperance movement to combat liquor, considered by the movement to be a societal destroyer. Religious zealot and teetotaler Reverend George Barrel Cheever subscribed to the school of thought that alcohol was the devil's medicine and a corruptor of man. Cheever, of Salem, wrote a short story detailing the ills of the distillery, "The Dream, or the True History of Deacon Giles' Distillery." At the time, Salem had four distilleries. Cheever wrote his story as an exposé of the detriment that alcohol production causes a community. In the story, the distillers are depicted as pure evil by their own merit. Cheever likens the family-owned distillery to the fiery pits of hell, where not only does the distillery create illicit liquids but also distills on the Sabbath! As the story progresses, a group of efficient, unpaid workers come in at night to help at the distillery. Giles locks them inside. Unbeknownst to Deacon Giles, the workers, who are actually demons, secretly inscribe on the barrels sayings describing the evil of the spirit, such as "a potion from the lake of fire and brimstone" and "insanity and murder." When the hogshead barrels of alcohol are brought to the taverns, customers frightened by the ghastly sayings bring the barrels back to the distillery. With so much unsold product, Giles's business was eventually ruined. Culling from history, the Deacon Giles Distillery in Salem is named after the distillery in Cheever's story.

This distillery story was published in 1835, and Cheever wrote a companion piece about Deacon Jones' Brewery with the same message, with demons brewing this time instead of distilling. In rebuttal, John Stone, a Salem distiller who was also a deacon, took Cheever to court over this glaring likeness to himself, as the details about Giles and Stone bore an uncanny resemblance to each other. Cheever was put in jail for only a couple of days and afterward wrote the brewery story.

One of the most notorious events in the history of Boston, one that led to a significant loss of life, had to do with a certain ingredient used in the distilling process of rum: molasses. A molasses tank with a 2.3-million-gallon volume owned by the United States Industrial Purity Distilling Company burst on January 15, 1919. This tragic event, known as the Great Molasses Flood of 1919, led to 21 deaths, over 150 injuries and property damage amounting to about $100 million.

Not only did New England's seaside location benefit the distilleries with exportation during the years of the triangular trade, but two centuries later, the ocean also became a source of illegal libation importation. The term *rumrunner* is used as the name for different New England establishments, including a *Rum Runner* boat in Newport, Rhode Island, and the now-defunct Rum Runners, a bar on Cape Cod. Rumrunning was popularized as a by-product of the illegalization of alcohol during Prohibition. The term comes from a supply of contraband rum or other liquor such as champagne, gin or even poor-quality whiskey, also known as "rot-gut whiskey," which was stored on such aquatic vessels as schooners or steamboats anchored in international waters in an area known as "Rum Row." Rum Row was situated outside the nation's boundary, between Cape Ann and Cape Cod. These ships carried the liquid gold from such faraway lands as Nova Scotia, Canada and even England. They would dock offshore, and under the black of night, smaller boats would meet them for their share of the illegal substances. Another way the ocean-faring New Englanders could subvert the Prohibition decree was through lobstermen, who would fill their traps with bottles.

Today's craft spirit industry in the Boston area is thriving. In addition to the distilleries that are profiled in this book, major Massachusetts breweries

The Vendome copper still at AstraLuna Brands. *Photo by author.*

have started distilling, including Tree House, which is known best for its prestigious beer. Even Martha's Vineyard–originated brand Black Dog, which mostly sells clothes (although it started as a restaurant and tavern), has its own line of rum. Clearly, craft spirits have moved from a small niche to public consciousness.

We will take a look into the distilleries that dot the landscape of the Boston area. From the islands and Cape Cod to the North Shore, come along for a distillery road trip. Learn about the different spirits being distilled at each location and about the team of individuals whose hard work goes into the craft spirits that we all enjoy. But first, let us investigate how spirits are made.

PART II

FROM GRAIN TO GLASS

The process of making spirits is the journey from a raw harvested grain to a delicious liquid by means of many different steps. The classification of each spirit differs mainly in what primary ingredient is being used. Rum comes from sugarcane (and is most often made from molasses, a by-product of sugar production). Brandy comes from fruit. Whiskey comes from grain. Vodka can come from a range of ingredients. Gin needs to have certain botanicals added, but overall, the actual distillation process remains similar from spirit to spirit. For this description of the gestational period of our spirit, the focus will be on whiskey making. But note that whether it is whiskey or rum, the overall process is the same. It's just that the starting ingredient and final product are different. American whiskey also often spends time being aged in barrels made of American white oak. While other spirits, such as gin, can also be aged, the aging process is most associated with whiskey and rum. The majority of craft rum producers use barrel aging. The big difference is that rum producers have the ability to use both new charred barrels as well as previously used barrels. There are always exceptions to the rule, though. White whiskey is an unaged version that one does not have to wait around for years to consume. This book will not describe the exact distilling process of each spirit, as it would, quite honestly, be tedious to many readers. Similarly, each distillery's process is also not elaborated on fully, as this would become redundant. For the sake of keeping it interesting for the reader, this section will focus on the distilling process for the layperson. No chemistry degree or prior distilling experience is needed to understand this.

John Stark, head distiller at Boston Harbor Distillery, leads a tour. *Photo by author.*

Whiskey making starts with the four main ingredients: water, grain, yeast and oak. The first part of the process begins off-site. Many of the Boston-area distilleries use raw grain from local New England farms in states such as Maine and New Hampshire. Two of the distilleries that use such grain are Short Path and Chattermark. The grain has to be saturated in a water tank, which leads to germination. Malting is the process of partially germinating the seed, then cooking it so that the grain does not completely germinate. At this point, enzymes become available that will convert starches into sugar. The most common and efficient malted grain is barley. Other grains can also be malted or left "raw" for added enzymes to achieve the starch-to-sugar conversion. From there, the grain needs to be milled for the grain itself to be broken open. The next process puts the grain into a large vessel known as a mash tun. Mashing is the process of converting starches into fermentable sugars. The first step is to cook the mash. Hundreds of pounds of grain are mixed in a mash tun. Next, the mash is steeped as one would with tea to break down the proteins and activate the enzymes, which break down the starches and sugars. Mashing the grain unbinds the starches. Grain and water are cooked to a specific temperature. Starches are essentially tightly bound chains of sugar. During this process, the starches unfurl, resulting in long chains of sugar. These long chains are chopped up by enzymes, creating fermentable sugar. The liquid that has been extracted is called wort. Once the starches are broken down, what is left is sugar water. For instance, at Boston Harbor Distillery, it is an off-the-grain fermentation. The liquid is strained, leaving the grain behind. The wort, which is a sugary liquid, is cooled down and then ready for fermentation. The grain is disposed of. The wort is then cooled down to about eighty degrees. The fermentation lasts about seventy-two hours. Yeast is added to the fermentation tanks, which Rhonda Kallman of Boston Harbor likens to Pac-Man eating whatever is in his path. Enzymes break down gelatinized starches into sugar. Sugar is then consumed by the yeast. The yeast's consumption of sugar is how alcohol is made. This is also the step in which the flavor of the spirit is created.

The yeast's by-product is a fermented alcohol known as wash. The wash is passed through the still twice. The first, or "stripping run," strips down the now-fermented wort. It strips the alcohol and leaves behind the water. Alcohol burns at 173.8 degrees Fahrenheit, significantly less than the 212 degrees that water does. It boils in the pot part of the still (when using a hybrid still, which many craft distilleries employ). A hybrid still is the most sensible for most craft distilleries, since they are often producing a variety of spirits. The alcohol is boiled in the still. In the condenser, the alcohol is turned into a liquid, called a "low wine." The plates of the still are not usually used during a stripping run. The still is cleaned out, and the alcohol is run back through. Many whiskeys are made using double-pot distillation. The next run through the still creates the "heads, hearts, and tails," which are cuts that the spirit is separated into. The heads are essentially poisonous and are thrown out. The hearts are the tasty part of the spirit to be enjoyed and consumed. The tails are not as potent as the heads but are still not for ingestion. Some distilleries will redistill the tails into another run. The alcohol level is then brought to barrel-entry proof, put into an oak container and allowed to sit. Interestingly, all whiskey comes out of the still clear; it is the maturation inside the barrels that gives it the distinct brownish hue.

Barrel proof has to be at 125 or below. For instance, if a spirit comes out at 160 proof, it goes through a smithing process to lessen it to 125 or below. To achieve bottle proof, the barrel-aged spirit needs to be cut with mineralized water. Bottle proof is much less than barrel proof. Take for instance Boston Harbor Distillery's Putnam Rye. At barrel strength, this sits at between 125 and 115 proof, but at bottle strength, it is only 80 proof.

Left: Measuring proof at AstraLuna. *Courtesy of Andrew McCabe.*

Right: The Lavender Bee's Knees cocktail at GlenPharmer Distillery is made from their Brookdale Gin. *Courtesy of Patrick and Beth Downing.*

As far as the aging process goes, Chattermark Distillers uses fifty-three-gallon barrels, which is the perfect size for the ratio between the surface area of the barrel and the spirit. A smaller barrel would not provide the same result. Although whiskey sits for years aging, the process from mash to barrel takes only about a week. When distilleries sell a product as "cask strength," it means it is taken straight from the barrel and has not been diluted with water. It will have a more robust flavor. For aged spirits, such as whiskey, the barrels are made from American white oak. For aging whiskey, this type of barrel is mandatory, but at other local distilleries, such as Privateer Rum, the same is used. Aging is dependent on the distillery. For instance, at Chattermark, its barrel releases so far are under two years, but moving forward it will not be releasing anything younger than two years old. Two years or older means the spirit can be designated as a "straight whiskey." This allows for the complex flavors of the wood to permeate through the spirit as it is able to mature through the extreme and temperamental temperatures that are found in New England due to the four distinct seasons. Most craft distilleries in the Boston area bottle their spirits by hand.

Along with how spirits are made, let us talk about a few of the products that are offered at Boston-area distilleries. Further investigation into the products can be found in the chapters dedicated to each, so consider this a flight of spirits to whet your palate in anticipation of the main course.

RUM

As rum was once an essential export from New England, it has once again taken a foothold in this region during the current wave of distilleries. Some styles are a throwback, paying homage to the rum of yore, such as GrandTen's Medford Rum. Others, such as Bully Boy's Rum Cooperative, blend their own with delicious rum from the Caribbean.

When mentioning the word *rum* in the region today, the distillery that comes to mind most prominently is Privateer Rum from Ipswich. Privateer distills a variety of rum of various strengths. One of the most coveted is that of the "Distiller's Drawer" series. The name is a nod to the fact that owner Andrew Cabot found that often the best rum was saved for the distiller's desk drawer. Privateer ages its rum in barrels of new American white oak. A taste of the Single Cask Rum reveals its complex character. The rum is aged in barrels for multiple seasons, and in the case of this specific single-cask rum, it is aged for five and a half years. The taste of this rum is complemented by a hint of vanilla from the aged barrel. At 114.8 proof, it is robust in flavor.

GlenPharmer seen from the outside. *Photo by author.*

AstraLuna Brands' Liberty Tree Boston Rum has a strong molasses nose, but the sweetness is mellowed in the taste. Directly opposite to this and Privateer's is the Reserve Spiced Rum from GlenPharmer. It is full of flavor and uses its Dark Tide Rum as a base. Nine spices are added to it: allspice, cinnamon, citrus, cardamom, cocoa, clove, Madagascar vanilla, nutmeg and pepper. The taste evokes the harvest time of the fall. It is the perfect autumn spirit as the weather grows colder and the days shorter. Bully Boy's Rum Cooperative Volume 1 is also sweeter in nature. At 84 proof, surprisingly, it has no bite to it, even in the finish. The sweetness evokes rum of the Caribbean with good reason, because, in addition to their own rum, it is blended with rum from Panama, the Dominican Republic, Trinidad and Jamaica. Deacon Giles's amber rum has the namesake hue due to the barrel aging. It has a pleasant nose to it. The taste is slightly sweet, with a small bite to it.

VODKA

Vodka is a spirit that most craft distilleries do not showcase as much as other spirits in their line. For one, a good vodka should simply be smooth, with no outstanding taste. The only trait I look for in a vodka personally is lack of bite. Additionally, vodka is most often used as a basis for cocktails instead of enjoyed neat. A few of the local distilleries do have an impressive vodka line. These include Dirty Water and GlenPharmer. Dirty Water has a vast array of vodka flavors to satisfy every palate. The clementine vodka has an orange taste, which makes it perfect in a vodka tonic. The horseradish vodka is an excellent base for a Bloody Mary. Others in the line include bacon, coffee and ginger as part of their current total of nine infused vodkas for their offerings.

Dirty Water distills its vodka from corn, whereas GlenPharmer, which also has a delicious line of infused vodkas, makes it from wheat. Along with their clean original wheat vodka, which is smooth, they have a variety of funky and yummy vodkas. The Bog Vodka is made with Decas Farms cranberries from Carver, Massachusetts. Its hue resembles cranberry juice, as it is a deep red color. The tartness of the berries shines through the wheat vodka base into a delicious creation. The Bean, which is a coffee vodka, has a full-bodied coffee taste, and Ghost is infused with ghost peppers, giving an electrifying twinge of heat. But it is oh, so appetizing.

GIN

Many of the Boston-area distilleries make a gin, and some make more than one. Take Short Path, for instance. In addition to their flagship gin, they also have a line of seasonal selections—Summer, Autumn, Winter and Spring gins—with ingredients reflective of the season. Speaking of naturally flavored gin, Dirty Water's Bog Monster is a gin made with local cranberries, giving the clear spirit a pinkish tint.

Gin is a polarizing spirit for many drinkers. Complaints of tasting like a Christmas tree are often heard. As more drinkers are exposed to excellent gin either by itself or in a cocktail, the number of gin fans is growing exponentially. The first gin I ever tried straight was from Nashoba Valley. This was the gateway for me to enjoy gin-based drinks. (A G&T is still a summertime favorite of mine.) Bully Boy's Estate Gin and GrandTen's Wire Works are two well-regarded regional gin favorites.

AstraLuna's Cape and Island Distillers makes the Sippewissett Cape Cod Gin. Named for Falmouth's Sippewissett Marsh, this gin is the base of some of their ready-to-drink cocktails, including the Sippewissett Gin and Tonic. Both the gin and the cocktail have an attractive image of a painted bird. The gin is a perfect base for a cocktail to enjoy on the Cape or anywhere to achieve that summer feeling.

Both Ryan & Wood's cask-strength Knockabout Gin and Deacon Giles's Original Gin are gins in the Old Tom style. The Knockabout has been aged in barrels that once contained their whiskey. In the gin's flavor, one can taste an oakiness. The Old Tom Gin has a dry flavor but not so much as a London-style gin. Deacon Giles's Original Gin is a play on "original sin," with the label depicting Adam and Even along with the serpent in the Garden of Eden. This is a smooth-drinking spirit. Their popular G&TAF, a ready-to-drink gin and tonic, is made from their Juniper Point Dry Gin.

Boston Harbor Distillery distills Lawley's gin, named after the George Lawley and Sons Shipyard, which was located where the distillery is today. It has a botanical mouthfeel and tastes so good going down. Short Path's gin series is reflective of the seasons. For instance, the Summer Gin is made from Maine wild blueberries. Short Path's flagship gin has a nice aftertaste, which I enjoy in lemon-based cocktails.

Although Privateer focuses on rum production, they also have gin as part of their repertoire. It is a seasonal release and is simply excellent. It is distilled from molasses, similar to their rum. It is considered "Tiki inspired," which

Left: Barrels aging at South Hollow Spirits / Truro Vineyard. *Photo by author.*

Below: Rhonda Kallman is CEO and founder of Boston Harbor Distillery. *Photo by Holbrooke Garcia.*

means the ingredients are reminiscent of those used in the Tiki era from the 1930s to 1970s. The botanicals include pomegranate, grapefruit, cinnamon, tropical fruit and spices.

WHISKEY

Although the Boston area historically is known for rum manufacture, more and more local distilleries are making whiskey. Boston Harbor Distillery and Working Man are both known as whiskey distillers, but many others have tried their hand at the American spirit. American straight whiskey, bourbon, rye and single malt are some of the types of whiskey that Boston-area distilleries create. Even white whiskey, which is essentially unaged, has its place in Boston, as it was the first whiskey put out by Bully Boy Distillers. Some distilleries will release a white whiskey while waiting for their other whiskeys to age. One of the region's most popular whiskeys is Boston Harbor's Putnam Rye. This is a straight rye with a full-bodied flavor. It is named for Silas Putnam, whose horseshoe factory graced the location of the current distillery. Another one of the most lauded whiskeys in Massachusetts is from Triple Eight. Their Notch Single Malt Whiskey, at twelve or fifteen years, is an award-winning spirit. Some area distilleries import their wheat from local farms in nearby states such as New Hampshire and Maine.

Dirty Water's Bachelor is a single-malt whiskey that is easy to drink. I taste a slight licorice element in it. Chattermark is also known for their whiskeys. Among their first whiskey releases is a white unaged rye that is often used as a backbone for their tremendous line of cocktails available in the tasting room. Their bourbon is the first of its kind to be produced in the city of Boston, from grain to glass. This single-barrel, four-grain bourbon is perfect in a cocktail or for sipping neat. Look for an array of new whiskeys to be released soon.

OTHER SPIRITS

In addition to the typical spirits of whiskey, vodka, gin and rum, Boston-area distilleries have branched out into a wide world of other spirits. One reason for branching out is that some distilleries have a bar. In Massachusetts, a distillery can only sell, even for on-site consumption, its own liquor. If a customer wants to order a cosmopolitan, the distillery must provide its own triple sec. Some distilleries think of creative variations of popular drinks, and some make in-house what they need. This is how Short Path started making triple sec. Not too sweet, their version has eclipsed their other spirits as their hottest seller. Similarly, Chattermark, not for public sale, but for their bar, has made a truly awesome liqueur from walnuts that is used in their Nochino. Short Path also makes harder-to-find (in New England) spirits such as ouzo, the Greek anise-flavored spirit. Amaro, a bitter liqueur, is produced at Short Path, which, just like their gin, has seasonally inspired versions as well. Other distilleries known for their Amaro include Bully Boy and South Hollow Spirits, the latter of which also has a chocolate Amaro on its menu.

One of the most sinful liqueurs has to be Boston Harbor Distillery's Maple Cream liqueur. This just may be the most delectable and decadent-tasting beverage I have ever tried. Perfect for a cocktail, it's so good that it can easily be sipped. At 30 proof, this has a rum base, but what shines through is the combination of real maple syrup and cream. Imagine a maple-based eggnog. Another interesting and just so tasty spirit is Dirty Water's Velnias. This is a spiced honey liqueur from Lithuania. I taste the honey and the cinnamon in an intoxicating blend. This is perfect when added to hot apple cider or just sipped. It is certainly more than just sweet, as the spices give it a robust flavor profile. This is another sneaky spirit, as it tastes as if there is no alcohol present.

READY-TO-DRINK COCKTAILS

Ready-to-drink cocktails (RTDs) have become an efficient and often delicious way to enjoy a favorite. Not all distilleries have jumped into this world, but many have. Some, such as Bully Boy and Boston Harbor, offer them as a bottled concoction. Take for instance the ready-to-drink espresso martini. Pouring one of these tastes like the perfectly crafted and balanced cocktail that a bartender just mixed up. Its sweet-to-strong ratio is spot-on, with the real espresso taste trumping any sweetness—exactly what I would want in an espresso-based drink.

AstraLuna has launched a few different brands of RTDs. From their Cape and Island Distillers moniker, they have such classic cocktails as a Cape Codder, a Mashpee Mule (where the brand is located) and a Gin and Tonic. They are all easy-drink, well-done replicas of the cocktail essentials. AstraLuna also makes the Par Tee line of ready-to-drink canned cocktails. With a golf theme (look at the name), the whole branding is based on the sport. Flavors such as the Transfusion, with vodka and grape juice, or the Half & Half, with vodka, iced tea and lemonade, are perfect gateway introductions for individuals who may be intimidated by or simply have not experienced the world of mixed drinks or hard alcohol. The flavors mask the alcohol bite completely; it would be hard to identify any trace of liquor in it. At 6 percent alcohol, they allow for easy consumption. Their Half & Half tasted more like a canned iced tea than a vodka-based drink.

Dirty Water Distillery also has a line of RTDs, including a Moscow Mule, a Gin and Tonic and even a Bloody Mary, which is the first of this cocktail that I have seen canned. They all have colorful, funky can art, which is worth the price of admission alone. At their original distillery location, they served their cocktails on draft as well and will presumably do so in their new home. Dirty Water has also forayed into the world of hard seltzer, with excellent results. Where too many hard seltzers are either bland or too sweet, Dirty Water was able to strike the perfect balance between the two in creating a seltzer that was still light but had enough flavor to differentiate itself from the pack. Distillery scene stalwart Triple Eight also launched itself into the canned cocktail world with the ever-popular Nantucket Blue and Nantucket Cran. The Nantucket Cran is delightfully refreshing, with that light and airy cranberry zing.

It's IMPORTANT NOT ONLY to understand where your local spirit originates and how it is made but also to be informed of the breadth of options available on the local market to help identify what fits your palate best. A traditional whiskey drinker may gravitate toward Chattermark's bourbon, but possibly after reading about Dirty Water's Velnias that same individual may want to branch out from their usual flavor profile. A great way to find out what you like is to visit the distilleries for yourself. The following section will give a long glance into the history of each of the region's distilleries. Take the time to go visit, sample and identify what flavors you appreciate. Enjoy the ride!

PART III

MEET THE DISTILLERIES

ASTRALUNA BRANDS

AstraLuna Brands, headquartered in Medfield, Massachusetts, has many different brands under its umbrella. These include Liberty Tree, Cape and Islands Distillers and Par Tee canned cocktails. Owner Andrew McCabe's role as the head distiller is certainly not the only job he does at AstraLuna. He is also the accountant, human resources director, payroll coordinator, quality control officer, graphic designer and sales representative, to name a few. Although AstraLuna makes a variety of spirits, including gin, apple brandy and ready-to-drink canned cocktails, the company is best known as a rum distiller, with offerings such as Cape and Islands Great White Rum and the Liberty Tree Boston Rum. Rum distilling in Massachusetts has strong ties with its history, as Boston and its northern environs were a hotbed of rum manufacture in the colonies and early days of the United States.

Business has always been in Andrew's blood. His family owned the McCabe Construction company based in South Boston, which he helmed starting in his twenties. Although he did not get into distilling until his forties, making alcohol has been a many-decades endeavor for Andrew. The first taste of home-brewed libation was from the batches of hard cider he fermented in his basement as a high schooler. Later, during college, he even brewed different styles of beer in his dorm room. As an adult, he began making wine in his basement in a self-made grotto. The wine making became a family affair, as he and his daughters would yearly crush the grapes from the crop's yield.

Spirits aging in barrels at AstraLuna. *Photo by author.*

The book *Chasing the Wild Asparagus* by Euell Gibbons was what initially turned Andrew on to the idea of distilling. The book deals with the idea of foraging for sustenance and finding natural medical remedies. The author elaborates on a double boiler used as a still. Andrew tried this with his wine, and it worked out well, much to his delight. He also was able to travel to faraway countries, including China, where he learned about the popular liquor Baijiu. He also traveled to distilleries domestically, which spurred his quest for distillery knowledge.

As head of the construction company, he employed Portuguese workers. They imparted their knowledge to him in terms of wine production and also Cachaça, which is a liquor distilled from sugarcane juice. Additionally, the group helped Andrew in terms of constructing his own still, where he then made brandy out of the wine he had initially produced. Throughout his journey, Andrew absorbed knowledge about distilling and making craft beverages in a number of ways.

AstraLuna was founded in 2013, with Cape Cod Great White Rum as the first spirit made. The company takes pride in distilling, using the best equipment possible, using superb ingredients and following good practices, thus creating a roster of liquor and canned cocktails that they are extremely proud of. The rum is aged six months and is filtered through carbon. In less than ten years, AstraLuna has created more than twenty products, all different from one another. The wide variety of libations means that there is an AstraLuna product for any consumer of spirits, from a refreshing canned cocktail to Boston-style rum. Visiting AstraLuna and actually trying the rum of different ages firsthand is quite the experience. One of Andrew's favorite parts of the job is being able to toast a customer with the product that he made.

Running a distillery is not just about crafting spirits and enjoying the ride. The business end of the operation is quite extensive. In addition to being head distiller, Andrew also manages many aspects of the company. To run a successful company, more than just understanding the science behind distilling is needed. Other skills are required, including the ability to learn computer programs in areas like graphic design. For instance, Andrew designs the cans of his Par Tee ready-to-drink canned cocktails. Invoking the golf theme (Par Tee for "party"), his label looks as if it is pulled right from a summer country club. Notice the awning on the Par Tee can? That pays homage to the awning and umbrella design at the Augusta National Golf Club in Augusta, Georgia, where the Masters Tournament is played.

Andrew is also adept at Adobe Premier, using a computer program for designing labels. Understanding the placement of the graphic design and how it will be best suited for the product is also important. In addition, a distillery owner needs to have a basic grasp of marketing. With the Par Tee drinks, Andrew's daughter advised him that the font size on the original cans was too small. He redesigned the label with a larger font, resulting in a more eye-catching image. With the responsibility of owning a company also comes creative control; therefore, Andrew was able to remedy the can design efficiently himself. One of the latest products Andrew submitted to the Alcohol and Tobacco Tax and Trade Bureau (TTB) is a Par Tee lime and lemonade flavor. A distillery has to submit the recipe, business plan, label, list of ingredients and name for each new product. The government replies with either a green light or a statement as to what needs to be changed and why.

Many of the bottle designs and logos for AstraLuna Brands, including the Liberty Tree and Cape and Islands brands, were designed by famed graphic artist Edward Stewart, who has also worked for such brands as Ben & Jerry's, Walden Local Meat and Hornstra Farm.

In addition to the Par Tee line of canned cocktails is the Cape Cod and Islands Distillers brand. These canned cocktails include the Mashpee Mule, Cape Codder, Sippewissett Gin and Tonic, Sweet Liber-Tea and Shark Bite. Along with the Par Tee line, these are perfect for sipping poolside or at the beach in the summer.

Even though Andrew is able to put his vast skill set to work every day, he does wish that eventually he would be at a place where his employees could cover the ancillary work that goes with his job, allowing him to focus on distilling. As the head distiller, his job is much more than a "set it and forget it" approach. He supervises each stage of the distilling process, from gathering the ingredients to placing the finished product in stores. Between the start and the finish, there are many other steps, including mashing, fermenting, distilling, barreling, blending, negotiating prices, packaging and shipping, all of which he oversees. Andrew enjoys being involved in all areas of the production process. "It's not entirely like I'm living the dream like pirates making rum!" He then laughs, "I mean sometimes it is!" When not distilling, Andrew can be found golfing, fly-fishing, target shooting or cooking.

Andrew also enjoys his role as a mentor in alcohol production in terms of distilling, as well as general business practices. One such example is the partnership AstraLuna has made with Babson College, a business school located in nearby Wellesley. One of AstraLuna's newer flavors is Faderade, in the Par Tee line. Tying in with the golf theme, a fade is a golf hit that causes the ball to fade from left to right. This vodka-based drink is packed with electrolytes, similar to the electrolyte-fueled athletic drink Gatorade. The students at Babson actually came up with this product idea, providing them with real-life business experience while in the classroom. Others in the Par Tee line include Half and Half, In the Ruff and Transfusion.

Try these spirits from AstraLuna Brands. *Photo by author.*

Another great product from AstraLuna, under the Liberty Tree brand, is their apple brandy. The apples come from nearby Dowse's Orchards in Sherborn. As Andrew puts it, "It's to die for!" The brandy is made with freshly produced apple cider. It is aged in barrels for anywhere between two and six years.

To explain the hierarchy of AstraLuna Brands, AstraLuna itself is the umbrella under which are Cape and Islands Distillers, Liberty Tree Distillers and Par Tee canned cocktails. Most of the distilling is done in Medfield. The company moved into its current location in 2018. The Medfield distillery is not open to the public, but a smaller satellite distillery and tasting room in Mashpee on Cape Cod for the company's Cape and Islands line are open seasonally in the warmer months. Most of the products under the Cape and Islands Distillery name are also made in Medfield, including its most popular, Cape Cod Great White Rum. AstraLuna also distributes for other companies, including O'Brien's Vodka, 5 & 20, HH Bespoke, Lola Mezcal and Chateau Suau wine.

AstraLuna distills in a beautiful Vendome Copper still made by the Vendome Copper and Brass Company of the bourbon mecca of Louisville, Kentucky. At first, Andrew tried making the Cape Cod Great White Rum in a different still before the Vendome was operational, but it just did not taste right. In Louisville, at a trade show for the American Distilling Institute, he met a salesman who turned him on to a specific yeast made for rum. Just a few days later, with the new yeast in the pot, the rum was perfect. Another spirit under the Cape Cod banner is Cape Cod Gin, made with local ingredients found on the Cape, including lavender, beach plum and rose hips.

Differentiating a craft spirit from those of the larger manufacturers is noticeable at first taste. A larger distillery is not able to take out the flavor imperfections that can be done at a small one. And if the batch is not up to their standards, craft distillers can redistill it. In distilling, there are three parts to the process: the heads, hearts and tails. The head is the first part of the batch. The heart is the middle, which is kept and has the most pleasing flavor. The tail is the remaining liquid. Andrew let me taste the difference among the heads, hearts and tails of a batch of rum. In sampling the heads and the tails, there is a profound taste differentiation. Heads are made of acetone, methanol, ethyl-acetate and ethanol, with an overpowering alcohol taste. The tails are also not something one would choose to drink. During Prohibition, the heads of moonshine were bottled as drinkable, which at times led to blindness due to the quantity of ethanol in it.

Andrew's favorite drink is a Manhattan made with his Liberty Tree Boston Rum. Made with sweet vermouth, orange bitters and a dash of Maraschino Luxardo liqueur, it is served either straight up or on the rocks. Both ways are delicious. Instead of the typical bourbon used in a Manhattan, he uses rum. Garnish with an orange twist and use real Luxardo cherries.

AstraLuna's rum is very dry, which is different from the products of the large rum manufacturers often located in the Caribbean. These companies tend to add a lot of sugar to cover the imperfections in the actual liquor. A drink for the bartending novice is their Great White Rum with a splash of lime. Andrew boasts that his rum is the "most sippable white rum out there!" This drink resembles a daiquiri without sugar.

AstraLuna is located on North Meadows Road in Medfield but is not open to the public. In the same complex as the distillery is 7th Wave Brewing and Farthest Star Sake brewery. The Mashpee tasting room and the distillery of the Cape and Islands Distillers is located at 10a Evergreen Circle in Mashpee. Visit them at www.capeandislanddistillers.com. AstraLuna can be found on the web at www.astraluna.com, Par Tee at www.drinkpartee.com and Liberty Tree Distillers at www.libertytreedistillers.com.

BOSTON HARBOR DISTILLERY

Of any distillery with the word *Boston* in its name, Boston Harbor Distillery lives up to its title. It is a brand built on history, both of the city and of the craft beverage scene in Massachusetts. The Boston Harbor Distillery is owned and founded by Rhonda Kallman, who, along with Jim Koch, started the Boston Beer Company, known to most of us as Samuel Adams. Beginning in her twenties, Rhonda has been at the forefront of the craft beverage industry for over thirty-five years. Her latest endeavor, which began in 2012 and opened in 2015, is the Boston Harbor Distillery. The distillery is located on a wharf in the Dorchester neighborhood of Boston. The distillery reflects centuries of history in a breathtaking brick-and-wood edifice. It distills a number of spirits, with an emphasis on whiskey.

Throughout the history of Boston-area distilling, rum was the most popular distilled spirit, created with molasses and supplied by the triangle

All smiles at Boston Harbor Distillery. *Photo by Holbrooke Garcia.*

trade, with the rum then exported to Europe and Africa. Whiskey is more closely associated with the southern United States in locales such as Kentucky and Tennessee, using grains easily grown in the region, including corn, barley and wheat. As Americans pushed farther westward, whiskey became the preferred spirit, using ingredients grown regionally. Just as distilling whiskey was rarer in New England in the early days of the country, this was also the case during the revival of independent distilleries over the last twenty years. The landscape consisted of vodkas and rums, but whiskeys were seen less frequently. Boston Harbor Distillery stands out for putting New England, and Boston in particular, on the whiskey trail. The production of whiskey here focuses on using whole grain products, which differs greatly from the manufacture of bourbon, a product many American whiskey drinkers are familiar with. Products such as rye and American single malt are substantial in taste, in part due to the grain, whereas bourbon is made from corn. This harkens back to Rhonda's tenure at Samuel Adams, where the brewery was looking for a full-bodied taste and used whole grains instead of corn, as other breweries were doing at the time.

There are a few different whiskeys that Boston Harbor distills. Most of their whiskeys are under their "Putnam" moniker, in reference to the building's former owner, Silas Putnam, and includes rye whiskey and the American single malt. In addition to whiskey, they also make rum, gin, liqueurs and distilled beer. Also available are ready-to-pour cocktails, including the Old Fashioned and the Espresso Martini. The rum is made of 100 percent molasses made in a New England style. The gin is wheat-based with some traditional botanicals such as juniper and coriander mixed with citrus fruits such as fresh oranges and tangerines. It is the perfect base for a summertime drink. The gin and rum are both under the "Lawley" name, named for the George Lawley Shipyard, another former tenant of the distillery site.

Only a few short years ago, today's distillery building was an abandoned warehouse. It has been preserved and renovated with expertise and precision. Rhonda's husband, Matt Shanley, is a contractor who had this vision for the building and is fully responsible for its renovation. His company is called Beach Island Construction. When Matt found the building, it was being used as storage space for a junk collector and was in a dilapidated state. With wood enveloping the interior of the building, my first thought was that it seems as if you have entered a gigantic whiskey barrel.

Rhonda Kallman's first love was whiskey. Even when Jim Koch asked her to help start a brewery, she said, "Gee, Jim, I don't drink beer; I drink whiskey." She had memories of her father drinking rye and ginger. Soon, though, she found herself at the forefront of craft beer in America. She became passionate about beer but even more so about the evangelism of it all, the education around the manufacture of beer. At that time, in the mid-1980s, the revenue from domestic beers in America was over $100 million, but the average consumer had no understanding of how it was made. It was as if the mass-marketed lagers simply appeared on the store shelves without anyone thinking about the actual process of manufacture. She learned then that craft was really an ingredient story. Although the word *craft* has been overused in the current day, it does mean quality ingredients and an authentic way of producing the said product. It is entrepreneurial and innovative. In one Boston Harbor bottle, all of those aspects come together. Rhonda gets excited about this process, with all facets of the craft movement converging to make one beautiful product. Even though alcohol has been her chosen path, at the root of it all, Rhonda loves entrepreneurship. But, she says, it's "hard as hell." It's even harder in the whiskey business than with other craft libations.

Rhonda Kallman.
Photo by Holbrooke Garcia.

Rhonda spent fifteen years helping Jim build Samuel Adams, making the brand a household name. After Sam Adams became public, Rhonda left the company. She later created her own brewery, New Century Brewing Company, which launched in 2001. "New Century" refers to the first brewing company of the millennium. Rhonda was inspired by Dr. Joseph Owades, who invented light beer, to start another beer company. The brewing company was launched on the eve of 9/11. The idea was to give craft-beer drinkers a light alternative. The beer was canned, which was ahead of its time, as most beer was bottled. New Century came out with a beer known as Moonshot, the original caffeinated beer. Due to the mixture of caffeine and beer, Moonshot was eventually banned by the FDA because of other companies' drinks, including Panther Joose and Four Loko, which also mixed caffeine and alcohol. These drinks were made with low-grade, higher-proof alcohol, artificial coloring and high caffeine content.

Rhonda lost her heart for the beer business and dissolved New Century Brewing. She realized there was a white space in the Boston area for whiskey making, so she started to look for a site for her distillery. She and her husband found a dilapidated warehouse on the Dorchester waterfront. She signed her lease on the location in 2012, although the doors would not open until 2015. Rhonda put in a small still to make small-batch whiskey.

Throughout history, brewing was done primarily by women. This was due to the fact that women tended to the needs of the household while the men were out fighting or hunting. In medieval England, women took their beer to local markets. To draw attention, they wore large pointed hats, like that of the traditional depiction of a witch. Additionally, they kept their liquid in a cauldron, not for a potion but for their beer. Cats were kept to help keep mice at bay, preventing the rodents from devouring and contaminating the grain. When the Protestant Reformation took hold, men decreed that women should not take on jobs such as brewing and instead should tend only to matters of the home. Men took hold of beer manufacturing and falsely associated female brewers with their pointed hats as witches, an image that has been forever ingrained into the persona of a witch. With the disparagement of women through the false association with witchcraft, men drove out the competition. From the Reformation on, women were removed from the alcohol-making processes and were expected to remain in the home doing domestic chores. Brewing became an entirely male-dominated field.

Even in the twenty-first century, Rhonda found herself, a female entrepreneur, a rarity in the field of alcohol making. Thankfully, the time of witch accusations is a thing of the past. But even today it is not easy. But for

Rhonda, standing out among her peers is "pretty cool." She reiterates what the statistics show, that it is more difficult to be a woman in this industry. Even with lots of experience, it is harder for her. In general, the whiskey business is difficult. And even with her résumé, an aspect of the business such as getting financing is more arduous for a woman. Rhonda is an inspiration for female entrepreneurs. Despite a greater acceptance today of women in business, men still dominate. Additionally, being in the whiskey game, many of Rhonda's national competitors are in states such as Tennessee, Kentucky and Texas, which are generally more conservative.

Although Rhonda is a trailblazer in this industry, she would rather be seen as an entrepreneur not classified by gender. (The product at Boston Harbor Distillery is so good that the customer won't care who is at the helm!)

As Rhonda was in the process of renovating the building, it dawned on her: Why not pay homage to the man who constructed the building, Silas Putnam? Putnam automated the process of making horseshoe nails. His uncle was the Revolutionary War hero Israel Putnam, who is said to have killed the last wolf in Connecticut, the state where he lived. Israel Putnam was born in Danvers, Massachusetts, and is known for his heroics at the Battle of Bunker Hill. Boston Harbor named its whiskey products, such as the Putnam New England Whiskey, after Silas. Putnam actually supplied horseshoe nails to both the Union and Confederate sides in the Civil War. He also invented the retractable curtain rod. There are actually horseshoes on display that are original artifacts from the nail factory. Rhonda was always fond of the horse imagery often used in whiskey branding. But she wondered how she could tie horses to the history of Boston. It was a fortuitous coincidence that she was to open her distillery in a former horseshoe nail factory! The design of the products melded history with her desired imagery. Everything is purposeful in the branding. Even the calligraphy in the letter *H* in the Boston Harbor Distillery logo is taken from an eighteenth-century map.

After its use by Putnam's industry, the building became the site of the Lawley Shipyard, where yachts that won the America's Cup were built. One of the award-winning yachts is depicted on Lawley's product label. Also in this building, minesweepers were built for World War II. Minesweepers are boats used to uncover underwater bombs or other explosive devices. Lawley had a government contract to build such ships to help with the American war effort. The Lawley name is used for the distillery's nautical spirits, which include gin and rum.

The last notable entrepreneur who held residence in this facility prior to Boston Harbor was Seymour's Ice Cream Factory. Seymour's inspired the confectionary line of liqueurs such as the maple cream and coffee liqueur. The former name was Seymour's; unfortunately, a winery was already using the same name.

Demon Seed is a whiskey that has garnered quite a reputation. The first person Rhonda hired was the late Dr. James Swan, an authority on whiskey and whiskey production. He imparted his knowledge to Rhonda, which influences the distillery to this day. Swan lived in Scotland and traveled the world. The master distiller at Boston Harbor was John Couchot, who formulated most of the products. He introduced the notorious Demon Seed whiskey by presenting it to Rhonda in a Mason jar. Although spicy is not typically a taste she prefers, Rhonda was blown away at the first sip. But she did not know how to fit a product like this among the premium whiskeys in the Boston Harbor line. The history of the horseshoe nail factory and the Demon Seed whiskey coincide where folklore meets fact. Saint Dunstan, while working as a blacksmith, was visited by the devil. The devil asked him to fit a new horseshoe for his horse. Although the devil was in disguise, Saint Dunstan was able to see through it. He shod the devil instead of the horse, causing the devil much distress. Saint Dunstan agreed to de-horseshoe him if he agreed not to enter any buildings with a horseshoe placed over the door. The horseshoes at Boston Harbor pay homage to its history as well as this parable. With the spicy goodness of the Demon Seed whiskey, it just may be the work of the devil! It is made with their unaged rye infused with scorpion pepper, Vermont maple syrup and fresh ginger. Try it in a Nail Biter cocktail at the distillery's tasting room.

In addition to whiskey, rum and gin, Boston Harbor Distillery has a series of spirits known as Spirit of Boston. This melds Rhonda's past and present, as these are actually distilled versions of Samuel Adams beer. Beers that have been used in this series include an India pale lager, a double black lager, stouts and a tripel. The latest release is made from the Octoberfest. By using the different beers, the spirit ends up taking on a life on its own, depending on the original beer. Although whiskey-like in finish and taste, this drink cannot be called a "whiskey," since it uses hops. Each of these is proofed at 84, a tip of the cap to Boston Beer Company, which was founded in 1984. Similar to whiskey, these spirits are aged. But they do not need to be in first-run barrels, so they are often aged in used whiskey barrels, and this imparts another quality of flavor to the spirit.

The spirit that Rhonda says started it all is the Putnam New England Single Malt whiskey. This is made with 100 percent malted barley, with roughly 20 percent of it roasted. The roasty flavor and chocolate-like essence are inspired by the chocolate factory once headquartered in nearby Lower Mills, another neighborhood of Dorchester. Due to the chocolate manufacturer, the whole neighborhood was known to smell like chocolate. I could think of worse things to have to smell every day! This whiskey is aged for four years in a barrel of new American white oak with Level 4 char, which equates to a fifty-five-second burn of the interior of the barrel. This is 100 proof and so smooth. There is a darker hue to the spirit due to the barrel aging. It is stronger proof than the Putnam New England Straight Rye at 86 proof. For those so inclined, Boston Harbor Distillery offers barrels for purchase. For instance, the barrel strength of the rye has been bottled anywhere between 108 and 131 proof. Not interested in buying a whole barrel? Luckily, the cask-strength Putnam Rye is also available by the bottle.

Boston Harbor Distillery distributes throughout New England and Upstate New York and has started expanding throughout the United States as far as California, Texas, Louisiana and Florida. Certain spirits are available only at the distillery, such as Spirit of Boston Octoberfest and Lawley's Small Batch Pear & Cherry Gin. In many fine Boston-area restaurants and bars, Boston Harbor's spirits can be found, including, but not limited to, Smoke Shop BBQ, Jasper White's Summer Shack, Galley Kitchen, Davio's and Cheeky Monkey. Truly, this shows the versatility of Boston Harbor's spirits, as the restaurants range from the fine dining at Davio's to the family-friendly atmosphere of the Summer Shack.

Although John Couchot may have helped formulate the original recipes for many of the spirits, the current head distiller at Boston Harbor is John Stark. As with many folks in the craft beverage world, Stark is a career changer. He was originally a financial adviser at Prudential. While there, he always had his eye on distilling. As he was on the phone with the fiftieth client of the day at Prudential, he was daydreaming, "What if I had a distillery?" As a lover of whiskey, distilling and spirits have been passions of his. He thought that possibly ten years down the line he would switch careers. But the way that John started at Boston Harbor is truly wild. He reached out to them on their website, and Rhonda brought him in. It turns out that they needed an addition to their small team. John enjoys making whiskeys at the distillery. A downside of this task is that the product requires time. Part of the distiller's job is tasting the whiskey often, as it matures over a few years. John determines when it is ready to be bottled. As a consumer, he gravitates toward whatever he is not working on currently. For instance, if he is making gin, he will stay away from that drink and be more partial to rum. He always comes back to the whiskey, though. Among customers, whiskey tends to be the best-selling product. One way to enjoy the distillery is by taking a tour, where various products can be sampled. The maple cream liqueur has become a hot seller. Even for the customer who has been brought along for the tour by a friend but who may not enjoy spirits, the first taste of the maple cream is mind-blowing. It's the spirit for the non–spirit drinker!

The room where the whiskey is aged was once upon a time the Dorchester Ice Cream Factory's cold storage. It is bound by a foot and a half to two feet of cork insulation. With a full HVAC system, the temperature can reflect what is needed for the whiskey's maturation process. Many different varieties of oak are used in the barrels, with white oak from such states as Minnesota, Missouri, West Virginia, South Carolina and Kentucky. The differentiation between the oak from each of these locales is palpable. Much depends on the climate and the processes of each state. Take the two very different climates of Minnesota and South Carolina and the same product placed in barrels of wood from these locales, and the end results are much different.

The distillery offers cocktails, tours and tastings, including the VIP whiskey tour and tasting. Here patrons are able to experience the full range of spirits that Boston Harbor has to offer in an intimate group setting and can take home a Boston Harbor Distillery shot glass. The tour begins in what is known as the "Map Room." While here, take a look at the many historic maps that line the walls. Locals and visitors alike will enjoy seeing the maps of Boston from various years. The most striking difference is seeing when Back Bay was an actual body of water, compared to today's geography after that neighborhood was created using landfill. Here visitors can taste a few different offerings from the whiskey line, including the Putnam Rye, which has been aged in red wine barrels, and the Putnam Single Malt. The intimate setting allows guests to have a running dialogue with the tour guide, who is often Rhonda herself or, sometimes, the head distiller, John Stark. Who better to lead the tour than those closest to the operation? Next, venture into the actual distilling space. See such components as the mash tun and the still. Boston Harbor Distillery employs a hybrid still made by Vendome Copper and Brass Works. Coincidentally, their first still has the TTB number 1776. How fitting! In the fall of 2022, they added another Vendome 500-gallon still to make more of the good stuff. Learn about the process of making spirits and see the by-hand bottling line. Here the group is given more samples, which may include Lawley's New England Harborside Gin and Lawley's Dark Rum. For the VIP portion of the tour, the group heads to the final destination, the barrel room. This room was once the freezer of the Seymour Ice Cream Company. Not only is it impressive, with a vast quantity of barrels seemingly everywhere, but the sampling here is also like no other, starting with whiskey straight from the barrel. Sit around to finish the tour and try other products, including the Demon Seed whiskey, the Espresso Martini, the Maple Cream, the Coffee Liqueur, the Spirit of Boston specialty line of spirits made from beer and the Old Fashioned. Even if you tend to shy away from heat, try the Demon Seed; it is truly unique and exceptional. The heat of the peppers is pronounced, but so is the sweetness, softening the peppers' wrath. A hot aftertaste is left, but only for a moment. The VIP tour and tasting is the full experience for anyone who wants to learn more about how the spirits at Boston Harbor Distillery are made, with a fantastic tasting of much of the distillery's repertoire. Visit the distillery online at www.bostonharbordistillery.com for more information, including signing up for this experience, currently offered twice on Saturdays.

Boston Harbor Distillery is also used as a space for weekly live music, wedding-related celebrations and corporate and holiday parties. Unlike most local craft distilleries, which are on the small side, Boston Harbor is big, so it is able to accommodate large events. Its large windows allow customers to experience a masterpiece of colors at sunset. In the summer months, the patio is open for drinks al fresco, but the brick-and-wood interior is inviting as a cozy hideaway during the long New England winters. It is located at 12R Ericsson Street in the Dorchester neighborhood of Boston.

BULLY BOY DISTILLERS

Bully Boy Distillers was the first craft distillery in Boston in the modern era. They have become synonymous with the city, as they create handcrafted spirits, including whiskey, vodka and rum. Owned and operated by brothers Will and Dave Willis, the company put Boston back on the spirits map when it opened in 2010. Its product became available on shelves the following year. Find out what makes this distillery unique and its products so darn tasty.

Bully Boy Distillers began as a culmination of a lifelong hobby pursuit. The brothers grew up on the Charlescote Farm in Sherborn, Massachusetts, southwest of Boston. The farm has been in their family for generations, as it was started by their great-grandparents. As children, Will and Dave moved to the family farm with their parents from a less-rural area of Sherborn. For a kid, the farm was the best thing ever. As Will recalls, it was "totally sensory overload!" The farm came from Will's mother's side of the family, so, on

The sign marks the entrance to Bully Boy Distillers. *Photo by author.*

moving there, his dad, as Will describes him, "was also like a kid in a candy store." Their dad was an Eagle Scout when he was younger and quickly got the boys involved in all aspects of the farm. Later on, their father helped the pair by investing in Bully Boy at an early stage.

Distilling has been a passion of Will's for a long time. When he was growing up, his family made apple cider from the two hundred or so apple trees on the property. It was not a commercial cider operation, but they made a large quantity of it nevertheless. The kids were in charge of the small farm stand that the family ran. In addition to cider, they also made ice cream on the farm. Even as a youngster, Will thought the idea of making something himself was exciting. "As a kid, it was great having a hand in something that you could consume and that tasted good. It was our introduction to eating local."

When the brothers were older, they began trying their hand at making hard cider, which was a natural extension of their cider operation. After reading and researching the topic, their next foray was into the distillation of the hard cider they made. The operation at this point was very low-tech. They essentially used a two-and-a-half gallon outdoor still with an outdoor propane burner. Will laughs, "It was pretty terrible stuff but it worked!" It did spark within them the do-it-yourself ethos that making their own food and drink was rewarding.

Over time, they refined the processes. The two brothers ventured into careers unrelated to distilling, but they were always entrepreneurs at heart, craving control over their own destinies and waiting for the right time to begin their next step. Will was in the real estate field, and Dave's career was as a lawyer. The change happened to the pair in their mid-thirties. With the 2008 recession, they both had a view of what life would be like if they were laid off. Luckily, neither was let go of his job, but seeing colleagues go through this tumultuous experience gave them a firsthand insight into the reality of unemployment. Will had recently had his first child, so the thought of losing his job was especially perturbing. Even during this time, he would go to the office and not have as much to do as in normal times. The troubled times led the brothers to pursue the path to becoming masters of their own destinies.

The brothers had a working knowledge of how to distill spirits. At that time, there was a growing interest in craft libations, mainly beer, but they chose the spirits route. When they got their license, they were the fifth in the state to do so. They had seen what the Harpoon Brewery had done in Boston so effectively, resulting in success as a hometown brand. Will and Dave wanted to be Boston's first distillery in the modern era to become synonymous with the city itself.

The name *Bully Boy* originated on the family farm. The brothers' great-grandfather had a workhorse named Bully Boy. The name comes from the expression "bully," as in the phrase, "bully to you," often said by Theodore Roosevelt. Also associated with Roosevelt is the idea of the bully pulpit as a way for someone in office to speak their mind. The word *bully* in his phrasing is something of high praise. Their great-grandfather was actually a friend of Roosevelt's in college. The name is a nod to the brothers' roots, as the farm was what got them interested in the distilling business in the first place. This led to their commitment to incorporate the farm as much as possible into their brand, including their logo, which is a horse—Bully Boy himself. In the distillery is a large mural that includes Roosevelt and their great-grandfather on horseback. Across from the mural is the photo that the mural is based on. The mural can be seen through the window behind the bar in the tasting room.

Their Sherborn farm consists of a small beef cattle operation. Corn is grown here for the cows to supplement their grass diet. Corn is also used in some of the company's spirits. They also grow juniper berries for gin. The brothers have held true to their original mission of keeping the operation rooted in the farm. In 2022, the farm yielded sixteen thousand pounds of corn flour. That sounds like a lot, but that quantity is about a month's worth of work at the distillery.

As far as the distillery goes, Dave is in charge of the distillation aspect of the company. Will runs the show on the business end, appropriate with his business school background. In the early days, Dave and Will managed all aspects of the company. They made their product from about 7:00 a.m. to 3:00 p.m. and then went around to businesses to try to sell it, self-distributing it. (Now they distribute through Horizon Beverage.) Although the two brothers are able to manage all facets, they stick to their areas of expertise for the most part. Will related that he and Dave found themselves butting heads in terms of distillation. Since then, Will offers thoughts on new products but is no longer involved in the actual manufacture or production.

Dave is the head distiller but cannot be at the distillery all the time. This is in line with the company's employment model, in which they try to promote from within. Bully Boy has a high rate of employee retention. Dave has two other employees who help out with the distillation at this point. Dave can often be found in the distillery, viewable from the tasting room, experimenting with recipes like a mad scientist. Another key figure at Bully Boy is Andy Gelb, who seems to do a bit of everything but whose title is operations manager.

In the beginning, the brothers did not have an organized tasting bar or distillery tours, but a natural curiosity happened organically. At the time they opened, in 2011, when they were the only distillery in Boston, random people would pop in, and the brothers happily showed them around. (Now the company is much larger, and tastings and tours are available for the public on a regular basis.) The company grew, and in 2017, they built a new facility across the street from the original. The original spot houses a pot still that is used for distilling gin as well as a location to age roughly seven hundred whiskey and rum barrels. The main building has a 750-gallon pot still and tanks; this is where the bulk of the production takes place. The main building also houses the tasting bar (44 Cedric Street in the Roxbury neighborhood of Boston). It is open to the public from Thursday through Sunday but is also available to be rented for private events any other day of the week. The tasting room has a cool speakeasy vibe to it. It is darkly lit inside, but pretentious it is not. It is housed within the confines of an unassuming old warehouse. The area across the street is also used for outdoor sipping in the warmer months and is the location for both public and private events.

In 2023, the company is expanding yet again. The initial expansion will add much more room to store aging barrels. A second phase is projected to showcase another tasting bar. They are also toying with the idea of a catering kitchen.

Even though the distillery itself is beautiful and inviting, this accounts for only about 15 percent of Bully Boy's business, which is primarily done wholesale with their distributor, Horizon. Currently, Bully Boy products can be found throughout the six New England states, but they do ship nationally, facilitated through a third party in Connecticut (shipping out of Massachusetts is currently not allowed). Bully Boy has expanded methodically, so they are not looking at a national market but have recently expanded to Upstate New York. (By the time you are reading this, the product should already be on the shelves.) They focus on their "backyard." There are four employees targeting New England markets, including Providence, Rhode Island; Portland, Maine; New Hampshire; and Connecticut.

Bully Boy has earned its reputation as a Boston brand, with many consumers considering them the spirit of Boston. One of the hardest aspects of any craft distillery is educating the consumer. The tasting bar has been a great way to let the customer try a product and note the difference from large macro-distilleries. Manufacturing in-house is important, too, differentiating Bully Boy from other regional companies that may just be a brand name without any manufacturing taking place in-house. The fact that Bully Boy has been open since 2011 is a point of pride, since ten years in the craft beverage world can seem like a lifetime. Their products are expertly made with consistency from barrel to barrel and batch to batch.

At first, the "Boston'" tag was a selling point, but consumers have developed a more refined palate. They look for quality over geography. This has helped sell Bully Boy in the stores. Restaurants, though, are a different story. A few years ago, restaurants felt more compelled to carry a few local spirits, possibly from pressure from the consumer. Due to COVID and other reasons, including being short-staffed, with restaurants struggling to keep their own doors open, the trend is to stock more of the larger brands than the craft or local spirits. Brands like Bully Boy have had to make a push to get their products back behind the bars at restaurants.

The labels on the spirits are refined but simplistic, nothing splashy, resembling more that of a medicine bottle than a brand vying for attention. At the same time, this regal approach is eye-catching. Boston's Fair Folk designs the labels. This agency is also known for its renowned artwork and labels for another Boston craft libation magnate, Trillium Brewing Company.

Initially, Bully Boy launched three spirits: a vodka, an unaged white whiskey and an unaged white rum. White whiskey as a style was gaining some traction in 2011 and 2012. Larger brands such as Jack Daniel's and Buffalo Trace had launched their own white whiskeys. At first, Bully Boy became known for its white whiskey. Soon, though, that category lost momentum with the advent of mass-marketed flavored moonshines. The white whiskey was a nice tide-me-over, as the style was becoming less in vogue until their first barrel-aged whiskey was released. The first batch of the American Straight Whiskey became available in 2014–15. Instead of speed-aging the whiskey to get the product on the shelves earlier, Bully Boy took the longer view and took their time with the aging process. They felt that this was their shot to earn consumer confidence. Instead of rushing it to the shelves, they waited until the whiskey was fully ready.

The whiskey is aged in 53-gallon barrels made of new American oak with medium char. The American Straight Whiskey quickly became the biggest seller for Bully Boy. Throughout the existence of Bully Boy, whiskey has been a best-selling category. With a 150-gallon still to begin with, they wanted to make sure they did not run out of product to meet the demand. The American Straight Whiskey's mash bill is 45 percent corn, 45 percent rye and 10 percent malted barley.

When Bully Boy launched their gin, gin itself was a hot commodity in the craft distillery scene. With gin, a distillery can make its own mark on the liquor. With vodka, the goal being a tasteless, odorless liquor, it is harder for a distillery to put its imprint on it. But it's easier with gin. While their barrel-aged products were maturing, Bully Boy was selling a lot of gin and vodka. Make sure to try the Estate Gin, as this is an easy sipper, whether neat or on the rocks.

Bully Boy also released a Boston rum, a barrel-aged rum launched around the same time as the barrel-aged whiskey. The name is a reference to the direct geography of Bully Boy but also a nod to the historic rum manufacture that encompassed the city in its early years. They use blackstrap molasses, in the same style as the rums historically made in the Boston area. If whiskey has become the new spirit of America, rum is the original spirit of America.

Bully Boy walks the fine line between artistic interest and commerce, between "do we like it?" and "can it sell?" The first ready-to-drink cocktail from Bully Boy was the bottled Old Fashioned, and this was before RTDs were in vogue. (This category would explode during the homebound pandemic.) Bully Boy launched theirs long before the pandemic, in 2015, and it continues to be a hot product to this day. They also offer a bottled Negroni and are in the process of making a bottled Manhattan.

A surprise hit for Bully Boy has been their Amaro liqueur. There are very few domestic Amaro producers. The first Amaro they launched had a well-rounded profile, not too bitter and easy to make into cocktails, but so delicious

Enjoy a drink at Bully Boy's tasting room. *Courtesy of Bully Boy Distillers.*

that it can easily be sipped neat. The second release was a Rabarbaro Amaro, which just means that rhubarb root acts as the bittering agent. These are spirits that cannot be found in many area distilleries and are one of the only ones in New England. The Amaro contains twenty-six botanicals.

There is a section of the Bully Boy company known as the Rum Cooperative. This is a different kind of concept. The rum is sourced outside. Bully Boy was given the opportunity to buy some amazing twelve-year aged rums and just couldn't say no. They brought in casks to blend the rum to their liking. There have been three volumes of this series as of this writing. This trifecta of rum has been a fun addition to their portfolio. This rum is utterly delicious! The countries whose rum is included in the blend are identified by a flower on the label. My favorite so far has been the first volume, but all are excellent.

Also in the works are two bourbons. They are barreled in bond, which means they are aged for four years and are bottled at 100 proof. They are unusual in that they are malted bourbons. They have unique and fun flavor characteristics. Instead of competing with large brands such as Maker's Mark, Bully Boy has put its own creative spin on bourbon. It is able to have more fun with this spirit than the companies that are committed to the creation of a single taste.

Will's favorite drinks include the bottled Negroni, the Amari, the Rum Cooperative Volume 2, along with the whiskey. After a long day, when he arrives home, he is ready to pour the ready-to-drink Negroni or Rabarbaro as a go-to. It doesn't have an intense alcohol by volume (ABV) and so is the perfect sipping cocktail.

Watch out for the new bourbons as they launch soon. The brothers' other brother, Chris, owns the restaurant Pammy's, located in Harvard Square. It, of course, has Bully Boy on the menu.

From the beginning of Bully Boy, the Willis brothers have utilized the history of their family in creating a company that would have made their great-grandparents proud. From selling vegetables and ice cream at the farm to running a premier Boston distillery, the Willis brothers' success comes from organization, patience, creativity and determination.

In your Boston travels, be sure to include Bully Boy Distillers on your list.

CHATTERMARK DISTILLERS

Opened in 2019, Chattermark Distillers produces finely crafted spirits in Charlestown, right in the shadow of the Tobin Bridge. The distillery is literally housed in a building located directly under the steel behemoth of a bridge. The distillery is owned by John Sorgini, a military man turned lawyer and craft spirits entrepreneur. The head distiller is Kyle Leclerc, who has been a distiller both near (Boston Harbor Distillery) and far (Oregon). The two form the backbone of this company, which makes incredible spirits that are easy to sip neat or enjoy as the basis for an excellent cocktail.

Chattermark Distillers began production in 2019, with the paperwork aspect of it in the works a year earlier. It takes a village, so they say, and giving guidance to John and Kyle have been visionaries from the realm of local spirits, including Rhonda Kallman at Boston Harbor Distillery, the Willis brothers at Bully Boy, the team at GrandTen, Short Path and Privateer, to name a few. Working with individuals at these companies provided John with much-needed information in the creation of his own distillery. Starting in 2019 does not seem to have been ideal, due to the pandemic, which shut down the planet a mere year later. When making whiskey, however, 2020 ironically provided a silver lining. Since whiskey is an aged spirit, John and Kyle were able to get to work producing it and were given the opportunity to age it while their distillery waited to open to the public. During COVID, beverage manufacturers in Massachusetts

Kassandra Laskarides about to prepare a cocktail at Chattermark's tasting room. *Photo by Jaclyn Lamothe.*

were considered essential workers, so John and Kyle were able to continue working through the bleakest months. With a large, airy space, they were able to stay six feet apart without issue. They were able to produce their spirits without outside distractions, such as the pressure to open a tasting room, when their beverage portfolio was limited.

Although relatively new, Chattermark is already winning awards at national competitions. Chattermark is a full grain-to-glass whiskey distillery. They do not source any liquor, only grain, which comes from Maine and other local New England farms. The grain-to-glass process takes place under their roof, including the malting, mashing and fermentation. A full description of the process is provided at the outset of part II. All spirits at Chattermark are double-pot stilled. The first time through, the pot still separates the alcohol from the mash and strips it. This is called the stripping run. The product is known as a low wine. The low wine is then distilled, which separates the spirit into heads, hearts and tails. The spirit is proofed and put into fifty-three-gallon charred barrels made of new American oak. Whiskey must be aged by definition in charred barrels of this wood. Chattermark uses fifty-three-gallon barrels, ideal for the surface-area-to-spirit ratio. The spirits are aged for at least eighteen months, but many of them are aged for at least thirty-six months. The composition of the spirits maturing in the barrels is altered due to the changing seasons in the New England region, and this influences the barrel's wood.

The white rye is made a little bit differently. It is run up the column. (A column is part of the still.) This falls into a different production category than the other whiskeys. Chattermark uses its white rye as a base for its gin. For the gin, they put in the white rye and macerate the botanicals in the pot.

Everything comes out of the still a crystal clear color; the barrel it is aged in gives the spirit the color. As with many products in the COVID-19 fallout, there was a massive barrel shortage. Typically, Chattermark Distillers uses Adirondack Barrel Cooperage from Upstate New York for their barrels but have had to look elsewhere due to the shortage. John lauds Joe and Kelly Blazosky for the high-quality barrels that come out of this cooperage.

As a whiskey distillery, they have had to wait for most of their products to be ready. John jokes that when making whiskey, a distillery can "open, make the whiskey and then shut the doors for three years." Although this might not be the best business model, ironically, opening in 2019 and facing the pandemic is exactly what happened. Luckily, this worked out for Chattermark, and recently, they have started to get their products into the marketplace, into bars and restaurants.

John is the owner/CEO/founder of Chattermark, and Kyle is the head distiller. Their distillery used to house Downeast Cider before that company moved to its current location in East Boston. Chattermark officially moved into the space in 2018. Kyle began distilling out West, where he said people in the distillery scene are a little more intense than in the Northeast.

John grew up on the North Shore, and his background is in the U.S. Air Force. After he left college, he was on active duty in the air force. He left active duty to attend law school but stayed in the air force reserves. The attacks of September 11 occurred while John was in law school, and this brought him back into active duty. He had to leave law school for a year that autumn and returned a year later to finish up. He was a corporate lawyer in downtown Boston as part of a national law firm. Every two to three years, he was deployed overseas. It was quite the juxtaposition between his high-rise law office with views into Boston Harbor and his tours of duty in the desert. He felt that something needed to give. His wife is also a lawyer and, he laughs, "is a much better one than I am!" Part of his law practice was dealing with small companies, and he found himself wanting to be on the company side rather than on the law side. He enjoyed his career as a lawyer but thought it was time to try something different. Explaining the move in careers, John elaborates, "Veterans and entrepreneurship go hand in hand."

John spent a couple of years researching how to open a distillery, going to bourbon school, figuring out what works and what does not, as well as how to put a business plan together. Finally, it was time to take action. He stopped practicing law and set out on his dream of opening Chattermark Distillers. John is currently still in the military. He and his family live in Boston, and he wanted his distillery to be within the city limits. The water is very good in Boston, and the commute for John is easy. Actually, the legal name of the company is Boston Distilling Company. When visiting their distillery, one can see the first barrels they used, with that name on them.

The name *Chattermark* has its own interesting backstory. The word is a NATO brevity codeword that John has actually used in combat scenarios. It means to switch frequencies, but its connotations are more about overcoming adversity and building resiliency—carrying on with the mission. The logo itself is a paper airplane flying away. It is modeled after John's air force wings, which depict a paper airplane over a compass rose. On the logo, the airplane is flying through a compass rose of grain. Wings in the U.S. Air Force identify the job someone has; they wear their wings as a badge. John's position as an air battle manager is identified by the wings.

Take a look at their label; there are lines on it. If it were folded, it would actually make the paper airplane in the logo. Chattermark is proud that they mash, ferment, distill and bottle everything on-site and in Boston, and also that the ingredients come from New England farms. Another fun fact is that Samuel Morse, of Morse code fame, is from Charlestown. The Chattermark bottle reads "Boston Distilling" in Morse code. The back of the bottle has John's kids' names in Morse code. The distillery literally puts their stamp on every aspect of the design! John reflects on his time in the air force: "Of course now it is all computerized, but before that, it was literally a radar with a grease pencil. When we started the distillery, we wrote on each barrel with a grease pencil." They still use a grease pencil on the barrels.

John had no prior experience distilling before opening Chattermark, although he was always intrigued by the art and science behind it. His foray into the distilling world came through the business. When starting it, he wanted to be challenged by something that he had never done before. John wanted to provide a product and not a service. He also wanted something that, at the end of the day, brings people together. Whether it was a dinner with colleagues in the law field or a dinner with his crew, everyone came together and had a drink, so he wanted to be in an environment that fostered that mentality and comradery as an underlying principle. That ideal was part of the core of why John wanted to forge ahead on the craft distillery road.

When asked what his favorite spirit is, John laughs and says, "Well, it's ours now!" But he acknowledges that there is a whole world of fantastic spirits out there. He enjoys the different flavor profiles of spirits as well as the various processes used in distilling. He is fascinated by the process of making whiskey or scotch that will change the flavor from batch to batch. He is also intrigued by the types of fermentation needed with certain strains of yeast and understanding the barreling process, how long the spirit should age in a barrel and where that barrel comes from. These are all part of the complex process of distilling. With the use of ingredients from New England farms, the terroir of their spirits is all local, from the Northeast.

John went into the distillery business with the mindset of producing whiskey and other spirits from grain to glass, meaning not starting with a product shipped here from the Midwest or somewhere else. John relates that perhaps having the doors shut for a year and a half due to COVID helped Chattermark with their from-scratch whiskey making.

Spirits aging at Chattermark Distillers. *Photo by author.*

To open a distillery, one needs to sign a lease, order equipment and obtain a serial number for the distillery application. During that time, John met with many other distillers and put an ad out for a master distiller. Kyle is from Boston and had never been head distiller before, but this presented him with a great opportunity. John and Kyle really hit it off, and John was impressed with Kyle's ideas. The role of head distiller gave Kyle freedom, but he also had a shared vision with John of what Chattermark Distillers should be. The two of them are joined by Sylvan Peter as the three original employees, but they are looking to expand. In mid-2022, Kassandra Laskarides was hired as hospitality manager.

When Kyle joined the Chattermark team, he was working in Oregon with a blending and bottling operation. His passion has always been creating things from scratch. He browsed the online forum and heard that someone in Boston was looking to start up a distillery. Kyle is from Salem, Massachusetts, and was happy to get back to his home. He first got into the industry while living in Santa Fe, New Mexico. He was working at a ski and snowboard shop after college. He looked at Craigslist for jobs and saw that Santa Fe Spirits was hiring. His first roles with the company included bartending and picking up wort in Albuquerque, which is about an hour's drive away. He was used as a utility man for the company and simply fell in love with the industry. Kyle puts it best when he explains why it is the perfect career for him: "For me, it blends artsy-creativeness with ditch digging, for the lack of a better term. I appreciate the creativity and the physical components of the job." His next career move was across the country at Boston Harbor Distillery, which he helped open. He worked there for two and a half years. After this, he moved out to Bend, Oregon, where he "mixed the life of a snowboard bum and a distiller." He then moved out to the wine region near Portland to help a blending and bottling operation get off the ground. He figured that Oregon, with its several distilleries, would offer more opportunities to further himself within the industry. But many of those distilleries are owner-operated, which meant less opportunity for Kyle to obtain his goal of being a head distiller.

Since collaborating with John on Chattermark, Kyle has learned so much within the last few years, including old-fashioned techniques and how to put quality first. He believes in using locally sourced products as much as possible, as John does. Procuring the grain from Maine, doing extended ferments through their stunning still and using the best barrels are illustrative of the ideals both men have. Kyle comes at distilling from an artist's angle but has had to learn chemistry through using yeast as well as the chemistry that

What shall I try first? *Photo by author.*

happens within the aging barrel, which develops all of the unique flavors. Kyle's favorite spirits are derived from fruit, such as Eau De Vie, which is a clear fruit brandy. For whiskey, he would just taste his own barrels.

The tasting room is set off from the main distillery and is an attractive, convivial space that is easy to raise a glass in. Their Single Barrel Rye Whiskey is double-pot distilled and is aged through four New England seasons, with the current offering aged twenty-two months. Aging through the seasons lets the spirit experience the changes in barometric pressure and temperature. As the pressure changes, the barrels breathe. Via cooperages such as Adirondack, the excellent spirit is allowed to age in a high-quality barrel. They are also beginning to make spirit mixers, which will allow them to serve an array of cocktails in their tasting room, since the only alcohol they are allowed to serve is what they make themselves. Their Pot and Column White Rye has a big taste, which, when enjoyed neat, is a surprise, since the clear color often has mellower connotations. The expectation of the clear liquid is much different than the realization, with fantastic results! For whiskey purists, drinking translucent whiskey is contentious; some need the brown, opaque quality. This won a gold medal in 2022 at the ADI International Spirits Competition in the category of best white whiskey. The rest of their portfolio in 2022 captured silver medals. Chattermark has become a family affair for John, as his children help pick the pine needles that are used for their coastal forest gin at Annisquam in Gloucester.

Not only did Chattermark have to create the spirits, but readying their tasting room was also quite the undertaking. Kyle states that the worst task that he had to do was paint the taproom ceiling. They also wanted to get a wall down to the brick foundation but had to grind through lots of layers of old paint. The build-out of the distillery took a year before any spirit was distilled. It is amazing to see what happens behind the scenes at a distillery. From the process of renovating the space, they were able to then have their hands on every detail of the space and were really able to understand it, from the boiler to the ceiling to all of the weird little quirks of the building. The process started in 2018. Their equipment was supposed to be delivered in late 2018 but did not arrive until the following year. Talk about a difficult task! When the equipment arrived, they had to take each item out piece by piece. They made the tables currently in the tasting room out of the pallets the equipment arrived on. With the costs associated with opening and operating a distillery, such as setting up the still and renovating the space, John and Kyle relied on themselves, as hiring out would cost much more. For other processes, such as plumbing and electrical work, they had to rely on professionals.

The tasting room has recently opened to the public. It is managed by Kassandra Laskarides. Before joining the team at Chattermark, Kassandra spent many years in the beer industry at Night Shift Brewing, with locations in nearby Everett and Boston. Stopping by the tasting room, guests are able to imbibe a variety of excellent cocktails made from Chattermark spirits. Similar to other distilleries that have a bar, Chattermark can serve only alcohol that is made in-house. For drinks such as a gin and tonic or whiskey and soda, it is not a big deal, since the nonalcoholic component (the tonic or soda in these cases) can be outsourced. But any drink that includes a typical alcoholic mixer such as triple sec or vermouth needs to be made in-house.

Kassandra has been experimenting with different recipes, with delicious results. One cocktail she serves is the Nochino Manhattan. The base is their white rye, but it also includes a walnut liqueur that they make in-house. Many of their drinks utilize white rye as a base, since Chattermark does not currently make vodka. Another tasty creation is made of rye, a jalapeño simple syrup, serrano pepper and lemon. This concoction hits on all notes. Starting with the slight pepper heat, it gives way to the tanginess of the lemon, which creates an unforgettable journey for the taste buds. The Charlestown Buck, a personal favorite, is bourbon based and includes a muddled strawberry, simple syrup, bitters, lemon and ginger beer. Its pink hue may seem to predict a sweet sensation, but instead it has a full mouthfeel that is highlighted by the strawberry and punctuated by the zing of the ginger beer.

Chattermark Distillers is the only bourbon and rye grain-to-glass distiller in the city of Boston. Additionally, its bourbon is the first ever mashed, fermented and distilled in the city. Making Charlestown proud, they are establishing themselves in the neighborhood, with Monument Tavern as their first restaurant customer. Branching out from there, Chattermark is making a name for itself both in the region and internationally by earning high accolades for its spirit line. The distillery is located underneath the Tobin Bridge at 200 Terminal Street in Charlestown. Drive past the well-known Charlestown Navy Yard, then enter what seems like an industrial lot and follow signs to the left for "200." As you approach the long warehouse building, Chattermark is the first business. The location is part of the fun. For the newbie, the area almost seems off-limits. There is on-site parking, as it is not close to public transportation. Visit them online at www. chattermarkdistillers.com for more information.

DEACON GILES DISTILLERY

Salem, history, demons and Liquid Damnation are just a few intriguing concepts to introduce the Deacon Giles Distillery in Salem. Culling its name from the foreboding nineteenth-century pro-temperance tale "Deacon Giles' Distillery," penned by abolitionist minister and writer George Cheever, this distillery combines history, lore and spirits (certainly apt for Salem) in an intoxicating blend.

In his short story, "The Dream, or the True History of Deacon Giles' Distillery and Deacon Jones' Brewery: Reported for the Benefit of Posterity," George Barrel Cheever tells the tale of a deacon, one Amos Giles, who, in addition to his deaconship, runs a distillery. Not only is he distilling liquor, the devil's drink, but he also is a malcontent who is terrible to his employees, pays them in spirits and distills on the Sabbath. In addition to spirits, Giles' Distillery also sold Bibles (a neon sign on the wall of the actual distillery pays tribute to this). The story goes that after his employees left, a group of mysterious individuals came to work for him. Giles locked them in the distillery, and they proved to be quite industrious. The workers were eventually found out to be demons, for in the barrels of libations

The story of Deacon Giles comes to life on the distillery's walls. *Photo by author.*

sent to taverns, inscriptions such as "Liquid Damnation," "Cholera" and "Consumption Sold Here" were invisibly etched on them, unbeknownst to Giles. The customers were too afraid to drink these, and Giles had to take back the barrels, destroy the rum and burn the barrels, forever adding an odor of brimstone to his distillery. The story of Deacon Giles was a jab at Deacon John Stone, a wealthy distiller in Salem. Stone sued Cheever for libel and won. Cheever was flogged in Salem and sent to jail for a short time. Still fervent in his belief, he went on to pen the story of Deacon Jones's brewery after his release but was eventually run out of town.

Co-owner and head distiller Jesse Brenneman relates that the story of Deacon Giles' Distillery is not well known. It seems that the only folks who know it either have the last name Deacon or are deacons themselves. This being Salem, many people assume that the Giles in question is a reference to Giles Corey, the farmer who was accused of witchcraft, along with his wife, and crushed to death by stones being piled on his body. He eventually uttered the famous last words "More weight." The interesting name of the distillery with a story unknown to most visitors makes for a good conversation starter in the tasting room.

Considering the area's history, what better point of reference for a Salem distillery than Deacon Giles? For visitors who do not know the story, it is a great talking point over a cocktail in the Speakeasy Lab. Indicative of the city of Salem itself, whose main aspect of tourism is due to the Salem witch trials, an unspeakable tragedy turned moneymaker, the tale of Deacon Giles adds a bit of fun and phantasmic flair to the modern distillery scene with its backstory and related branding. Co-owner Ian Hunter discovered the story of Deacon Giles when he was volunteering on the *Friendship of Salem*, a replica of the *Friendship* sailing vessel built in the city in the late eighteenth century. Both Ian and Jesse worked together at the Harpoon Brewery in Boston. Ian was a homebrewer before his job at Harpoon but worked as the controller for the brewery. Jesse was a brewer at Harpoon.

Jesse and Ian became good friends in part while working together at a homebrew contest held by the company. The brews are voted on, with the winning beer made into a large production batch. Over time, they got closer while hanging out after their shift in the Harpoon employee lounge. They realized that they both hoped to open a brewery someday. Their skill sets complemented each other well, since Jesse could manage the production aspect while Ian could manage the business end. After considering opening a brewery, they realized the beer market was becoming a bit saturated and decided to pursue opening a distillery instead.

A few months into creating their business plan, Ian traveled to Bermuda with his wife. They were drinking the famous Rum Swizzle at the historic Swizzle Inn in Hamilton. While sitting on the beach outside, it dawned on Ian, "The Boston area has a rich history of rum, so why don't we do a distillery?" Returning stateside, he sold the idea to Jesse. Jesse thought that a distillery would present a new challenge for himself and would be part of the emerging craft industry. After the business plan was completed, they had to find a space in which to settle. They found their current spot at 75 Canal Street in Salem. After the zoning and financial processes were complete, Deacon Giles Distillery opened to the public on, of all times, Halloween weekend 2015. Given Salem's rich spooky history, what better time to open than the city's busiest weekend!? Jesse calls their coincidental opening date "a perfect accident."

The first two spirits that Deacon Giles launched were the Liquid Damnation, a white rum, and the Original Gin, which is a botanical gin. (You may remember the words *liquid damnation* as one of the warnings etched on the barrels in the Cheever story.) The white rum is 100 percent molasses based, made in the traditional New England style. This style is a nod to the

Salem-based rum distilleries of yore. Fun fact: at one time, Salem had nine distilleries in town (at a time when the population was much less than it is today). Originally, Deacon Giles planned on barrel aging this rum, but it tasted so good coming right off of the still that they decided to stick with that. It also led to a differentiation between the white rum and the amber rum they eventually released. The composition of the gin is based on the preferred flavors of Ian and Jesse.

A year later, Deacon Giles released their spiced rum, called Friendship's Bounty. Its inspiration, and hence the name, was the *Friendship* vessel, originally used in the spice trade. They used spices that would have been found in the holds of the ship. Instead of the modern baking spices often used in spiced rum in such products as Captain Morgan and Sailor Jerry, their rum used ingredients including cacao, orange peel, long pepper and a little bit of Tahitian vanilla. Long pepper at one time was the most popular pepper in the world. It grows in a few select spice islands near present-day Indonesia. Black pepper ended up replacing long pepper in popularity, as it was able to grow in more varied climates.

The next spirit they launched was a vodka, Yankee Ingenuity. At first, they hesitated to make vodka, since as a distiller it is not a very difficult or crafty spirit to make. When they decided to make it, they had a few requirements. They wanted to make it gluten free and for it to have a backstory. Many white rums are made with pure cane sugar, so they wanted to use this ingredient. They decided to start with a white rum–based recipe using the cane sugar but to distill it into a vodka. The end product was delicious. It is also a nice option for those who lead a gluten-free lifestyle.

The next chronologically in their spirit line is the amber rum, called Solera Costera. Amber rum spends a minimum of eighteen months in barrels. At Deacon Giles, they age this rum using a Solera aging method. It is a rare process stateside; it is popular in Portugal and Spain and used for the creation of dessert wines such as port and Madeira. This process is different from most rum production. When the barrel of rum is ready, it is harvested, but only half is bottled. The other half is put back into the barrel. The next set of barrels is opened to refill the missing half from the first set. It is a three-tiered system in which the rum is moved down the line every time it is harvested. It lends itself to a high level of consistency and a unique flavor profile of the barrel-aged rum. Not only does it have great taste and is a cool story to tell, since not many American distilleries use this method, but there are also significantly fewer barrels used in this process. Most distilleries fill the barrel and then empty it entirely for bottling.

The still at Deacon Giles Distillery. *Photo by author.*

The next spirit (as of this writing) is the Juniper Point Dry Gin. Once a vodka, which is the base for most London dry gins, is made, Deacon Giles uses the same botanicals (juniper, coriander, cardamom, orange peel, lemon peel, angelica root, mace and rose hips) as the Original Gin but in different proportions. Recently, Deacon Giles Distillery has added two absinthes to their repertoire.

At first, the distillery did not have a license for pouring cocktails. They were approved on Repeal Day, December 5, 2016, celebrating the anniversary of the repeal of Prohibition. Once the license was granted, Deacon Giles branded their bar area as the Speakeasy Lab. The opening of the bar enticed locals and tourists to come in, enjoy a craft cocktail using the Deacon Giles spirits and connect with the brand and space. Previously, merely selling their products and offering a taste made it difficult for patrons to fully embrace the brand.

On a first visit to Deacon Giles, walking down to the lower level Speakeasy Lab can be likened to descending into hellfire. But if this is hell, heaven can wait! Note the "Bibles for Sale" sign when entering. The Speakeasy Lab is a comfortable room. The space is adorned with cheeky fire-and-brimstone imagery from the pages of Cheever's story, so it is easy to sidle up to the bar for a drink or enjoy it at a high-top table. There is a second space, dubbed the "tiki bar" in the summer and the "ski lodge" in the winter. It even comes equipped with a tiki-themed portable bar. Live music is played here at times, as the space is used for many purposes.

Since the opening of the Speakeasy Lab, the community has been able to connect with Deacon Giles, enjoying a cocktail at the bar. In turn, the distillery does much for the community at large, including raising money for hurricane relief in Puerto Rico and Black Lives Matter and even hosting "Dolly Parton parties," where customers bring in books to donate to a local organization that promotes literacy and brings books to kids on the North Shore. (Dolly Parton is known for her work promoting children's literacy.) In 2017 and 2019, the distillery won "Best of the North Shore" in *North Shore Magazine*.

Asking Jesse the favorite spirit he makes, he laughs and says, "Usually the one I'm drinking at the moment!" Speaking of drinking, Deacon Giles Distillery offers a line of canned cocktails, including the perfectly balanced "G&TAF" which is a gin and tonic, a mai tai, a vodka cranberry and a rum mule. Jesse says that the two spirits he drinks the most are the Amber Rum and the Original Gin.

Deacon Giles Distillery continues a long-standing tradition of distilling in Salem and is the first distillery to open in the city in two hundred years. Built on history, with branding and ingredients that recall a bygone era and a bit of Salem lore, it is also a thoroughly modern and fun place to enjoy a fantastic cocktail made with the utmost care. Visit them at 75 Canal Street in Salem or online at www.deacongiles.com.

DIRTY WATER DISTILLERY

Entering through an iron gate emblazoned with the Dirty Water logo, you'll know you are in for a memorable experience. The distillery opened in America's Hometown of Plymouth, Massachusetts, in 2013. At Dirty Water, expect a fine selection of spirits, many designed with locally sourced ingredients. Dirty Water is known for their variety of flavored vodkas, from the conservative (clementine) to the outrageous (bacon). They also distill whiskey and rum, as well as liqueurs such as limoncello. Try their Bog Monster gin made with local cranberries, or the spirit that put them on the map, the Velnias, a Lithuanian honey liqueur known as a Krupnikas. Not only a distillery, their tasting room also encompasses the sister brand of LlamaNama Beer Labs. Local company Leyden Street Coffee shares the space. Also look for a selection of hard seltzers and canned cocktails to go at Dirty Water. Come in for a sample or a cocktail and purchase some items for your own cabinet.

Dirty Water tries to keep everything as local as possible. For the vodka and gin, the process starts with a semi-spirit that is redistilled in-house. One aspect of the vodka that separates Dirty Water from the pack is the array of flavors they come in. Food-forward flavors permeate their vodka, including horseradish, honey, cranberries, cucumber, bacon and more. All are created by using the actual food item and not an extract or syrup, as is typical of many distilleries.

The name *Dirty Water* did not originate with the nearby Boston phrase representing the Charles River, the Red Sox or the region. Ironically, the Town Brook, which flows just behind the distillery, was the source of the fresh drinking water so desperately needed by the Pilgrims and a primary reason they chose to stay in the area. The name derives from the fact that it is illegal to home-distill ethanol. When the fermentation process was complete, speaking in code, founders Pepi Avizonis and Steve Neidhardt would say, "I've got some dirty water, are you available to clean it up?" (it is legal to home-distill water). In addition, the name does have a reference to the Boston area.

Velnias, a Krupnik or Krupnikas, is a liqueur that is one of the top sellers at Dirty Water, for good reason. Not only is it extremely tasty, but also its story is interwoven with that of Dirty Water's owner, Pepi Avizonis. Pepi's family (their name is spoken as "Krupnik" in Poland and "Krupnikas" in Lithuania) is of Lithuanian descent, so the Velnias is known as Krupnikas. Krupnikas is a popular alcoholic drink in Lithuania. For me, this is the spirit

Left: An Old Fashioned made with Privateer Rum. *Photo by Reagan Byrne.*

Right: Try the White Hot cocktail at Chattermark Distillers. *Photo by Kassandra Laskarides.*

Left: A Negroni at Deacon Giles Distillery. *Courtesy of Deacon Giles Distillery.*

Right: The Raising Arizona cocktail. *Courtesy of Deacon Giles Distillery.*

Above: John Stark, head distiller at Boston Harbor Distillery, leads a tour. *Photo by author*.

Right: Dirty Water Distillery's head distiller, Brenton MacKechnie. *Courtesy of Jaclyn Lamothe*.

Opposite, top: Rhonda Kallman is CEO and founder of Boston Harbor Distillery. *Photo by Holbrooke Garcia*.

Opposite, bottom: Meet Andrew McCabe, owner and head distiller of AstraLuna Brands. *Courtesy of Andrew McCabe*.

Top: AstraLuna's Liberty Tree rum. *Photo by author.*

Middle: The Spirit of Boston line. *Courtesy of Boston Harbor Distillery.*

Bottom: The GrandTen family of gin. *Photo by author.*

Top: The Lavender Bee's Knees cocktail at GlenPharmer Distillery is made from their Brookdale Gin. *Courtesy of Patrick and Beth Downing.*

Middle: The Cranberry Mule, made with GlenPharmer's Bog cranberry vodka. *Courtesy of Patrick and Beth Downing.*

Bottom: Tiki Drink made with Privateer's New England Reserve Rum. *Photo by Reagan Byrne.*

The Vendome copper still at AstraLuna. *Photo by author.*

Left: The Charlestown Buck, a personal favorite! *Photo by Kassandra Laskarides.*

Right: Try the Putnam Single Malt Whiskey! *Courtesy of Boston Harbor Distillery.*

The still at Bully Boy. *Courtesy of Bully Boy Distillers.*

The stories-tall still at GlenPharmer Distillery. *Photo by author.*

The still at GrandTen Distilling. *Photo by author.*

Left: Warm up with some Northern Comfort. *Courtesy of Justin Pelletier.*

Right: Ten Mile River Rye Whisky is modeled after George Washington's mash bill. *Photo by Kelly Lendall.*

Whiskey, anyone? *Photo by author.*

Left: The Ryan & Wood lineup. *Photo by Kendra Dott's Double Exposure.*

Below: Ready for a boat ride? *Photo by Beth Crowell.*

The still at South Hollow Spirits. *Photo by Joe Navas of Organic Photography.*

The bar at Short Path. *Photo by author.*

Boston Harbor Distillery from the outside. *Photo by Tommy Colbert.*

Left: Charring the barrels. *Photo by Max Kelly Photography*.

Below: Toasty. *Courtesy of Adirondack Barrel Cooperage*.

Left: GlenPharmer's Spiced Rum cocktail. *Courtesy of Beth and Patrick Downing.*

Right: Privateer Palmetto (also known as a Rum Manhattan). *Photo by Reagan Byrne.*

Left: Chattermark's Nocino Manhattan. *Photo by Kassandra Laskarides.*

Right: Measuring proof at AstraLuna. *Courtesy of Andrew McCabe.*

GlenPharmer seen from the outside. *Photo by author.*

Liberty Tree Boston Rum in Boston. *Courtesy of Andrew McCabe.*

Yum, Velnias! *Courtesy of Jaclyn Lamothe.*

that stands out the most. The honey base mixes with a cinnamon taste. The recipe used at Dirty Water is a family heirloom, passed down to Pepi from his grandfather, who immigrated to America from Lithuania at the end of World War II. The traditional recipe uses grain alcohol, which can be rough on the palate and takes about a year to settle. Dirty Water uses a refined vodka, which can be processed in three days. The sweet taste stems from the fact that it is made from 17 percent honey. Only a handful of other distilleries are making such a honey liqueur, and they are all located on the East Coast. Currently, only one distillery per state is distilling this concoction. Other states include New Hampshire, New York, North Carolina and Pennsylvania.

At Dirty Water, everything they create starts off as a grain, such as corn or barley, except for the rum, which starts off as molasses. The initial distilling process is the same as that used in making beer but takes it a step further. For Dirty Water's rum, they use table-grade molasses and evaporated cane juice. Other distilleries use blackstrap molasses, which can create a harsh and biting rum that Dirty Water chooses to stay away from. They choose to use the evaporated cane juice over refined sugar, due to its pliability. As head distiller Brenton MacKechnie states, "The refined sugar ends up not behaving as well as the evaporated cane juice." Their whiskey from start to finish uses a two-row barley and local malt. At Dirty Water, they try to use as many local ingredients as possible. For the vodka, a halfway spirit is used. This is a common practice for vodka and gin in many distilleries around the country, although some, such as Silver Bear Distillery in Dalton, Massachusetts, start this process from scratch. This halfway spirit is carbon-filtered and redistilled.

One area of vodka production that sets Dirty Water apart from their competitors is the vast array of flavors they use. They use food either before or during the distillation process to impart the flavors. Many other distilleries prefer to use an extract or syrup instead of the actual food item. The companies that use those methods add the syrup or extract after the distillation, which changes the flavor of the final product. The only spirits that contain sugar are the liqueurs that are part of their makeup. This would include the use of a local honey from Billerica, Massachusetts, which, for example, is used in the Velnias. The cranberries that are used for both their cranberry liquor and Bog Monster gin are locally harvested in Sandwich, Massachusetts. The cranberries give the traditional liquid a pinkish hue. The one ingredient they shy away from locally is the bacon for the bacon-flavored vodka. Brenton jokes, "Then we'd be taking locally raised bacon out of people's mouths, and that's not fair!"

I moved to Plymouth in 2014. Walking around the downtown area, I noticed an intriguing metal gate emblazoned with a logo that read "Dirty Water." (The door is actually a piece of scrap metal that Pepi etched the logo onto with a plasma torch.) On further investigation, I found out that this was a distillery. During their infancy, Dirty Water did not keep regular hours. It was open as long as there was someone to staff it. In trying a few of the spirits, including their first three, Velnias, What Knot rum and a plain vodka, I could tell that these stood out from the pack. In 2014, Dirty Water introduced their first gin, the Bog Monster. A year later, the amber rum hit the shelves. And in 2016, the Bachelor, a single malt whiskey, arrived. Nosh Tavern, a former Plymouth restaurant, had a partnership with Dirty Water. Instead of infusing their own vodkas in-house, Nosh proposed the idea of certain flavored vodkas such as the clementine and horseradish to Dirty Water, which they still make to this day. Brenton explains, "The bacon vodka was done as a sort of joke." The coffee vodka is made with freshly roasted dark roast Columbian coffee from Speedwell Coffee, also located in Plymouth.

Around 2011, owner Pepi was at a family gathering. All the husbands were sitting around a table shooting the breeze. A family bet started over who would get into the production business first. Pepi and his brother-in-law Steve Neidhardt liked the idea of a brewery, but they were popping up everywhere and there wasn't much room for growth. Pepi and Steve started experimenting on their own.

Brenton began his career at Dirty Water Distillery in 2015, working only Saturdays. Steve left Dirty Water and Massachusetts in general to move out to Washington in 2016, pursuing altogether different dreams. Pepi alone did not have enough time to focus on the distillery, as he had another career. Steve had been in charge of the rum, and he left a large hole to fill. At the time, Brenton had just started getting into the sales side of the business. Soon after, their sales representative left as well. In November 2016, Brenton changed his career to work full time at the distillery. He previously worked in pharmaceuticals, eight years as a chemist in a lab and a few years in quality assurance dealing directly with FDA requirements. Both aspects of his prior work would help him immensely in running the distillery. Whereas in the craft libation industry many individuals begin as complete hobbyists, Brenton brought with him the mix of chemistry and experience with regulatory agencies, both necessities in running a distillery. He even had to deal with audits in his previous line of work, so he had an idea of what to expect. In addition to his mastery as a distiller, he brings with him the organizational skills to help the business side of Dirty Water run smoothly.

Another fan favorite at Dirty Water is their limoncello. This uses the whole lemon instead of lemon extract. The lemons are soaked in a high-proof vodka. By this method, the end product is 80 proof. I asked Brenton what his go-to spirit is at Dirty Water. He said it depends on his mood. The most versatile to him is the honey liqueur, the Velnias. Using it in coffee or tea or creating a "grown-up" apple cider are all fun applications. It can also be paired with rum to make a hot toddy. Some folks use it for cooking as a glaze for ham or scallops. Other customers have used it to make Bananas Foster or crepes. It has also been paired with the nearby Plymouth Bay Winery's wines, creating yummy wine-based cocktails. It also can even be paired with beers. Making a martini with the coffee vodka and the Velnias is another approach to this versatile beverage. A sour in the summer with simple syrup and some lemon juice is a good use. The dark spices and honey of Velnias create depth that makes it adaptable to many different uses.

Riding the hard seltzer wave, Dirty Water Distillery cans their own versions. Unlike many mass-marketed hard seltzers, which bring to mind fizzy flavored water, the ingredients of Dirty Water's permeate through their product. Brenton elaborates, "Our goal with whatever product we make is that it would be something that we as consumers would want."

The road to serving full drinks in the tasting room was an arduous one. The licensing was tricky, since both liquor and beer (from their sister company, LlamaNama Beer Labs) is served under the same roof (although there are different rooms for liquor versus beer). The ability to enjoy full pours began on one of Plymouth's biggest days, the Fourth of July. The parade route marches right past the former location of the distillery, and the distillery opened its doors that morning, making it a perfect parade-watching destination with drinks on the ready to serve the revelers. Once the tasting room opened in this capacity, drink sales surpassed bottle sales. Through the long months of the pandemic shutdown, only to-go bottle and can sales were available. Even after the tasting room reopened, bottle sales still eclipsed on-site drink sales.

Prior to LlamaNama Beer Labs being brought into the Dirty Water fold, the now-defunct Plymouth Beer Company was housed here. Whereas Plymouth Beer Company was a separate entity located inside Dirty Water Distillery, LlamaNama is within the same company but technically run as a separate entity due to legal stipulations. In January 2017, Brenton and Pepi floated the idea of creating an in-house brewery, making Dirty Water a one-stop shop. Some customers do not drink hard alcohol, so the idea was to appeal to the folks who prefer beer. They were approached by Tom Frizelle, who wanted to start his own brewery. He operated under the moniker Plymouth Beer Company but eventually left. They wanted to keep going with the brewery idea. LlamaNama started small, with the intent of growing organically. In their original location, they took over an adjacent room in the building for their brewery. Legally, they had to have two separate service areas.

Leyden Street Coffee began as a service company restoring and repairing antique coffee equipment under the Leyden Street name. They entered the Dirty Water banner through personal connections with an employee. Leyden Street wanted to explore whether Plymouth could handle two roasters (with Speedwell Coffee also in town) and two coffee shops (along with Kiskadee Coffee). Considering the crowds at Leyden Street, the answer is a resounding "yes." This relationship has also worked well for Dirty Water, as customers who initially come in for coffee make return trips to the distillery or brewery. Word of mouth and social media are the two ways Dirty Water's name is spread, as they do not pay for advertising. The testimony of customers is a far better endorsement than paid advertising.

Dirty Water also benefited from their space. The original location was in an uber-cool former garage that had open-air seating in the summer and wonderful proximity to Plymouth's commercial and historic sites. The site offered all kinds of drink under one roof, from whiskey to coffee and seltzer to beer. Currently, the new location of Dirty Water is also excellent, right on the coast and housed in an old warehouse in the shadow of a sprawling mill complex.

For a smallish town, Plymouth is a craft-lover's dream. It has five breweries, two wineries, a distillery and a cidery, all within its confines. The community spirit here is unmatched. Instead of competition, each business has found its niche with the utmost respect to one another. Consumers do not have to pigeonhole themselves with one brand. Instead, they are able to sample all the variety of beverages available in America's Hometown. Plymouth has shown an affinity for diverse consumption.

Dirty Water Distillery was originally located at 10 Water Street in Plymouth. They moved to Cordage Commerce Center (colloquially known as Cordage Park), a former factory complex that was the largest employer in Plymouth in its heyday. The Plymouth Cordage Company was world renowned, as it was the largest rope and twine manufacturer on the planet. Currently, the former factory is home to restaurants, medical offices, a small museum, a winery and satellite campuses of local colleges.

Dirty Water's new location at Cordage Park is a craft beverage mecca. Along with the distillery and brewery, Leyden Street Coffee also moved here. Additionally, the 1620 Winery (named for the year the Pilgrims landed in Plymouth) is located next door, creating a true imbiber's dream. When approaching the Cordage Park complex, these businesses are not located in the main factory but are instead housed in the former warehouses at the rear of the sprawling brick building. During the summer, there is an outdoor restaurant called the Stack Shack, which offers yummy food in a beer-garden atmosphere. It is situated behind the factory on the waterfront and close to the distillery. The name refers to the 210-foot smokestack that unfortunately had to be taken down due to safety concerns in 2022. It stood proudly for 123 years. Leyden Street Coffee has a second location at 709 State Road at the Clement's Marketplace Plaza.

A visit here can be an all-day affair. In addition to the distillery, this is also home to their sister brand, LlamaNama Beer Labs. During the morning, stop by for the best cup of coffee in town. Under the same roof, there are tastes for every palate, from a maple oat milk latte from Leyden Street to a strong ale from LlamaNama. Try a sample of any of Dirty Water's spirit selection and enjoy a craft cocktail or a hard seltzer in the tasting room. There are bottles to purchase, merchandise, canned cocktails, beer and hard seltzer to go. Visit Dirty Water on a summer weekend, and you can see firsthand how popular this uber-cool distillery is. The address for the distillery is 49 Cordage Park Circle in Plymouth. Find them online at www. dirtywaterdistillery.com.

GLENPHARMER DISTILLERY

For a whole new spin on the distillery experience, make your way to GlenPharmer Distillery in Franklin. This distillery is located in a beautifully refurbished former factory building that wows even before you take a sip. The distillery's owners, Pat and Beth Downing, have taken a piece of history, a circa 1883 textile mill called the Brookdale Mill, and put a modern spin into the old space with their craft distillery. Stepping into the building, you see that the attention to detail is astounding. Not only a tasting room and a bar, GlenPharmer also has a whole restaurant, complete with an all-encompassing menu made in their scratch kitchen. With an event space upstairs, the building serves many functions. And, of course, their spirit lineup is truly spectacular. Most recently, the space was used as the Italian restaurant Incontro. For the unknowing customer, a visit to GlenPharmer is a different kind of distillery experience. Along with the restaurant, the venue itself evokes a sophistication, but one with an air of friendliness. The come-as-you-are ethos of a craft distillery is housed inside a beautifully refurbished nineteenth-century industrial space.

Pat and Beth, although not distillers themselves, are certainly knowledgeable about the process, due to their chemistry backgrounds. Beth is originally from Indianapolis, Indiana, and Pat is from Lee, located in the Berkshires in western Massachusetts. The couple met as lab partners at Purdue University as undergraduates. After graduation, Pat took over his father's family pharmacy in Lee. The couple moved to Franklin in 2007.

Prior to opening the distillery, Pat attended Moonshine University in Louisville, Kentucky, and had the arduous task of visiting distilleries near and far to see what he and Beth liked and disliked about distilleries in preparation for starting their own. Talk about difficult field research! Opening a distillery had been a dream of Pat's for a long time. The name *GlenPharmer* has a threefold meaning. Glen is a geographic reference to the valley in which the mill building is located. Historically, needing the natural water source, mills were located on rivers, as were distilleries. The small valley has the Mine Brook bubbling through. The distillery is lovingly detailed inside and out. There is a covered bridge over the brook, which GlenPharmer uses for

The GlenPharmer experience is like no other in greater Boston. *Photo by author.*

outdoor seating. Also look for the 1939 Ford antique truck parked in front, used as a focal point of sorts for the distillery. Looking at the mill in pictures evokes serenity and a step back in time. One would be surprised to know it is close to chain stores and restaurants such as 99 Restaurant across the street, a cell phone store and a storage facility. The location is the best of both worlds, as it is seemingly located in its own small world but is also only a two-minute ride from Interstate 495.

The second aspect of the name, the "Pharmer" element, comes from "farmer." As Massachusetts and other states post-Prohibition were promoting alcohol production, they were actually doing it to promote domestic agriculture. Hence the reason the licenses that distilleries are required to have in Massachusetts are for "farmer distilleries," even if there is no farm on the premises. The third aspect of the name, "Pharmer," is in reference to the "farmer distillery," but it is spelled with "ph." This "pharmer" aspect comes from the professions of Pat and Beth, both pharmacists by trade. The only hiccup has been from the Scotch Whiskey Association, which feels the name *Glen* has to relate to Scotland (think Glenfiddich, Glenlivet or Glen Moray). They can use the name *GlenPharmer* for all of their spirits except their whiskey.

Try the Bog cocktail at GlenPharmer Distillery. *Courtesy of Beth and Patrick Downing.*

Looking closely at their future whiskey label, the *e* is removed in "Glen" and replaced with three red swishes. One of the other obstacles that GlenPharmer had to face from the Alcohol and Tobacco Trade and Tax Bureau was the "pharmer" aspect of it. An alcohol cannot promote medicinal qualities. Changes had to be made to the label as a result, but the name was allowed to be kept. The logo was changed from the original, which was "GlenPharmer" in larger font and "Distillery" in smaller font, to "Distillery," also in larger font, so that no one would confuse the distillery with a pharmacy. On the original logo, at the end of the *R* in "GlenPharmer" the trailing *r* had an *x* through it, creating "Rx," as in a prescription. Historically, this stood for recipe, as it listed what was in the medicine. Fun fact: the antique truck's sign does include the *x* at the end, since it was made before the logo change. I guess this means these spirits are good for you, pharmacist's orders!

The Downings' distilling story begins in 2004, when Pat was in the Caribbean. A hurricane hit, and power was lost. He walked to a nearby restaurant each night, and each meal was chicken and fresh, locally grown vegetables. Additionally, there was no ice, but there was whiskey. At that time, Pat's drink of choice was Cabernet Sauvignon. (Now, Scotch-Irish whiskey, tequila and bourbon are his drinks of choice.) Around 2007, Pat tasted his first American whiskey and was shocked at how good it was. Previously, he thought all great whiskey had to be made in Ireland or Scotland. That got him wondering if he could be successful in the United States. Pat and Beth talked about it for years. In 2016, the couple visited Ireland to tour distilleries. Doing "difficult field research," they toured roughly seventy-five distilleries before opening their own. After taking the weeklong course at Moonshine University, Pat was ready to start. Luckily, their current building was put on the market. Although they were incorporated in 2018, the timing of their opening was ill-fated, as the distillery was slated to open to the public just as COVID stopped the world. Even with their current success, GlenPharmer still distributes their spirits, as they did from the beginning, in the old-fashioned way, pounding the pavement and going store to store with their product.

Even though the full GlenPharmer experience is simply spectacular, without having the product to complement the space, the distillery idea would be null and void. Never fear. Their lineup is amazing, so let's take a sip! Their vodka is distilled from wheat instead of the typical corn. The smell and taste of the vodka is a bit sweeter than most. There is an essence of wheat to the taste, and it is smooth to the palate. In reference to his products, Pat abides by the adage, "If you can't drink it neat, with no mixers, no ice, and can't enjoy it, then we don't want to produce it." All of the spirits at GlenPharmer certainly can be described this way and more. "Drinking it neat" is the gauge they use when crafting spirits. Each of the spirits at GlenPharmer has won at least a silver medal or higher at competitions. Beth chimes in, "We are so proud of what has been accomplished so far." Tasting the vodka on its own, the hint of a wheat taste makes it just a bit different than most, but it still has a smooth, clean finish.

In GlenPharmer's repertoire is their GlenQuila, their take on tequila, which many craft distilleries in America do not make. It is distilled from 100 percent Blue Weber Agave with the extract imported from Mexico. In taste, it is lighter than a typical tequila. Of course, Massachusetts is a far ride to Mexico, so they are not able to harvest the agave themselves. The yeast used is also imported from Mexico. The name *GlenQuila* is used, since tequila can only be from the Jalisco and other regions of Mexico. If a product says "tequila," it has to be imported from Mexico. If a local distillery makes it, it has to be from the region, but it could be redistilled or barreled locally. The GlenQuila was a double-gold winner in the New York World Wine and Spirits Competition. Along with a slight pepper note, there is a fruit essence to it as well. It is a reposado, which means it is aged for six months in used tequila barrels.

The Dark Tide Rum is another fantastic option in their spirit selection. The rum is distilled from two different types of molasses. The rum is aged, giving it a bit of a whiskey character. Currently, GlenPharmer is aging their whiskey in barrels of American oak, so using this in a traditional whiskey cocktail such as a Manhattan works well as a substitute. Both the smell and taste are absolutely delicious.

Their Reserve Spiced Rum is so tasty, with an incredible amount of flavor. The Dark Tide Rum is used as a base for the spiced rum, and then nine spices are added to it. The spices are allspice, cinnamon, citrus (mostly orange), cardamom, cocoa, clove, Madagascar vanilla, nutmeg and pepper. This rum is a double award winner, winning double gold at the New York World Wine and Spirits Competition and at the San Francisco World Spirits

Competition, and it is in the running for "best in class" in the San Francisco competition. When sipping the spiced rum neat, there is absolutely no alcohol taste to it. The taste evokes harvest time of the fall. It is the perfect autumn spirit as the weather grows colder and the days shorter.

The Brookdale Gin begins as a wheat vodka with eleven botanicals added. Many of the herbs that are used are fresh, as they also appear in recipes for the dishes in the restaurant. The botanicals include fresh cucumber (which is also used in the scratch kitchen), lemon zest, elderflower, chrysanthemum blossom, rose hips, hibiscus flowers, juniper, lemongrass, lavender, coriander and foraged pine needles. Originally, GlenPharmer was going to do a summer and winter gin, with the summer as a lighter floral bouquet and the winter as a heavier recipe. Instead of two separate gins, the Brookdale is a nice balance between the two. It is floral up front and, as the sip progresses, finishes with earthy tones. The taste progression becomes more pronounced as it is tasted, presenting a complex flavor profile that differs from many gins. The initial taste is very different from the final product.

As this is Massachusetts, an obvious choice for a fruited vodka is the cranberry. While most vodkas may have a hint of cranberry flavor, Bog, GlenPharmer's cranberry vodka, is like drinking a glass of perfectly balanced cranberry juice. It is actually their biggest seller. The base for the Bog vodka is the wheat vodka, which automatically gives it a bit of sweetness. With the added cranberry, the sourness and the sweetness balance each other. It still has the zing that cranberry lovers crave, certainly unlike any other cranberry vodka out there. Made from real cranberries grown by Decas Farms in Carver, Massachusetts, it won "best in category" from the American Distilling Institute. Carver is one of the major cranberry-growing locales in the nation. The drink's hue is a deep red, not a pink like that of many cranberry spirits. For a super easy cocktail, put Bog in a glass over ice, add lemonade and enjoy.

Bean is a recent addition to their spirit line. Although the restaurant has delicious food, it is essentially a tasting room, which means GlenPharmer can only sell the spirits they create. Given popular cocktail offerings, they have been able to see where holes are in their lineup and what customers are asking for. One ingredient that had been lacking was a substitute for Kahlua. Thus Bean was born. On first smell of this coffee-infused vodka, it is as if the imbiber has been transported to a coffee shop. It is made with coffee from Atomic Coffee Roasters of Salem and Madagascar vanilla. This is yet another spirit that can easily be sipped neat without the need for any mixers. Originally, distillers Marco and Alex made this for their house bar, but on first sip, Patrick and Beth knew this had to be bottled. Quite honestly, it tastes like an espresso martini without extra ingredients. Try it neat or on the rocks. Pat guesses that soon this will become their best-selling spirit.

Ghost is the most interesting spirit in their portfolio. It is a vodka infused with ghost peppers. Pat and Beth happened to watch the Boston travel show *Chronicle*, which profiled a farmer named Rooster Fricke. He grows hot peppers at his farm, Nobska Farm in Woods Hole on Cape Cod. Rooster is known for growing fantastic hot peppers. Years later, Pat contacted Rooster about collaborating on a project for the distillery. Rooster invited the Downings to his farm to spend the day. Pat and Beth settled on using ghost peppers for the spice and vodka for the spirit. They did not want to sacrifice flavor for pure heat. The process of tasting this spirit is unique. On first taste, sweetness pervades, but the sweet soon dissipates into heat. The hotness lingers, too, which makes for a perfect sipper. There is no need to rush this one. Beth enjoys a Ghost in Soda for a cocktail. She also enjoys a Bloody Mary, where the peppers interact beautifully with the vegetable base. This has won double gold and "best in category" twice from both the American Distilling Institute and the San Francisco competition. The San Francisco World Spirits Competition is a gold standard in spirit judging.

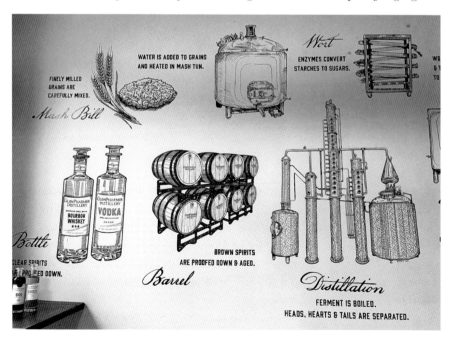

A science lesson while you sip. *Photo by author.*

The whiskey, which will be in bottles by the time this title is in print, is currently being aged. GlenPharmer offers a private barrel program in which individuals or a group can purchase a barrel of whiskey to be aged to their liking. Their names are then emblazoned onto the barrel program wall near the hallway leading to the tasting room. Among the more popular cocktails offered at the bar are their smoking cocktails, including the Smoking Volcano and the Smoking Gun. The Smoking Volcano includes the Ghost vodka, pineapple, chili threads, lime and Ghost guava BBQ. The Smoking Gun is made of Bean, Dark Tide Rum, orange and ancho-coffee bitters.

For some visitors, the distillery is simply an afterthought. As Pat puts it, "They think this is just a restaurant with a couple of stills in it." The restaurant itself is actually the tasting room of GlenPharmer but has a scratch kitchen attached to it. The restaurant brings a whole other demographic to the distillery. Foodies who may not be interested in beverages can still find their way here based on the rave reviews of the cuisine. Some folks come for the food and stay for the spirits; others come for the spirits and stay for the food. It's a win either way. Lunch, dinner and Sunday brunch are served. The menu is extensive, from soups and salads to sandwiches and entrées. Just a sampling includes salmon, steak and an array of flatbreads. Of course, you can order a flight of spirits in a sampler, enjoy a specialty cocktail or try a spirit neat or on the rocks. The restaurant has been able to supplement the distillery, especially while waiting for aging spirits to be ready. A restaurant is a complicated endeavor by itself, but it has been able to complement the spirit side of the business. As Pat discussed, regarding the idea of the craft movement in general, "It is nice, because people get to experiment, which causes it to be interesting."

For a newer distillery, GlenPharmer actually has the largest production capacity in the Northeast, utilizing an eight-hundred-gallon and a five-hundred-gallon still. Although they currently do not need this large a capacity, one complaint that distilleries they visited had was that their stills were too small and needed to be upgraded. By starting off on a larger scale, GlenPharmer hopes to eliminate the need to grow, at least for a while. The food element started as a way to draw people into the distillery before they knew the product or the brand. While spirits aged in barrels, GlenPharmer was able to start on the path toward recognition. They felt that with a great chef creating interesting food, this would be an initial draw. The hope was to create a social atmosphere combining eating and drinking, along with a sense of community. The idea is for a polished, casual experience where customers can have a nice meal but not have to get dressed up to do it.

GlenPharmer has a barrel program for those interested in purchasing one. *Photo by author.*

The tour of the distillery takes visitors into the production room, the barrel room to see the spirits during the aging process and, finally, the sampling room, where visitors can enjoy tasting the array of spirits. GlenPharmer is a multifaceted distillery experience for the craft libation fan, the foodie and the history lover—or all three. GlenPharmer is located at 860 West Central Street in Franklin, Massachusetts, and online at www.glenpharmer.com.

GRANDTEN DISTILLING

GrandTen Distilling, based in South Boston, is owned and operated by Matt Nuernberger and Spencer McMinn. With homage to the past with such products as their flagship Wire Works American Gin, GrandTen gives a nod to the history of the building where the distillery is housed, a former iron foundry. Another tip of the cap to Boston spirits of the past is their Medford Rum. Rum made in Medford was said to be the finest in the land during the heyday of rum distilleries in greater Boston. This rum is concocted in the traditional way of New England rums of yore, using pure blackstrap molasses.

GrandTen is located in South Boston. *Photo by author.*

GrandTen was started in 2010. Before beginning the distillery, Matt enrolled at Babson College in 2008 for a degree in business with a focus on entrepreneurship, with the goal of starting a company. With unfortunate timing, the market crashed in the fall of 2008, so there were no internship opportunities available for this budding businessman. After a period of introspection and reflection, Matt asked himself, if he could do anything at all for his career, what would he do? That is when he decided to create a craft distillery. He spent the summer of 2009 researching and understanding how to make his dream of a craft distillery become a true business. He learned what it would take to get started in this industry. The idea of GrandTen Distilling headed toward reality in 2010, his final year at Babson.

Matt soon realized that this operation would be bigger than himself. Around the same time, his cousin Spencer McMinn had finished his PhD at the University of Virginia. A busy time in his life, Matt had also recently gotten married. For his honeymoon, the couple traveled to Paris, where his cousin was living at the time. This is where he approached Spencer about starting a distillery with him. After a couple of weeks mulling it over, Spencer was in. Matt graduated from Babson in May 2010, and Spencer and his wife moved from Paris to Boston a month later. Soon they raised the needed funds and incorporated. In looking for a distillery space, the duo wanted to make sure they opened in the urban center of Boston. A year later, they finished their licensing and officially opened their doors in 2012.

GrandTen makes quite the body of spirits, including rum, brandy, gin, whiskey, vodka and cordials. Their mantra is "quality first," which was their initial goal. The distillery is well regarded for their product, which is still made in small batches. As Matt explains, "There are no robots or computers here; the work is all done by hand." GrandTen's slogan is "Made in Boston with pride." Matt relates that the spirits they make are what they themselves want to be drinking. As a result, they take great pride in the quality and taste.

Matt has always had a passion for spirits. He also likes the creativity allowed in crafting spirits. Instead of beer or wine, which has a narrower flavor focus, the range of spirits is vast. "If it has sugar in it, you can ferment it and turn it into a spirit," Matt points out. "The flavors you can add to it are totally different from what is usually used in beer and wine." He found out that the spirit world is much larger than that of beer and wine.

GrandTen is known for its Wire Works Gin. *Photo by author.*

Matt has a science background, helpful in understanding the concept of distilling. Spencer has a chemistry background. Despite the fact that distilling has existed for thousands of years, they were undaunted in their efforts to fully understand its concepts. They approached distilling with a scientific mindset.

Matt's favorite spirit at GrandTen is the Wire Works Special Reserve, a barrel-aged gin. This gin is unique. Gin is typically unaged, so barrel aging the gin in whiskey barrels is an uncommon approach. This tasty gin works in many capacities, including as a whiskey replacement. It is fully botanical but with mellower notes of whiskey. The whiskeys at GrandTen are also different from most, as they are part of a rotating selection. Their South Boston Irish Whiskey is actually distilled and aged in Ireland and imported into their facility in South Boston and then blended, creating a unique concoction. This whiskey is almost always available and consistent in taste, whereas their whiskeys made in-house vary, with each barrel being different.

Their Medford Rum is a tip of the cap to the region's past. This was one of the first products that GrandTen set out to make. After learning how to make rum, Matt and Spencer enjoyed their first batches, but it was not quite what they envisioned as Medford or New England rum. Instead of the full-bodied dark rum of the Northeast, the initial runs tasted like Caribbean rum. After investigating their methods, the men realized that they had been using traditional Caribbean rum yeast and methods. They had to research and dive into traditional rum-making methods of New England. One discovery was that yeast had not even been discovered until halfway through the lifetime of Medford's rum age. People at the time may have known that putting a hot liquid outside could distill it, but yeast itself had not yet been identified as an organism. With that knowledge, Matt and Spencer went back to the drawing board, or the pot still, and decided to use a yeast that would have been found in the air during that time in history. Although they did not use spontaneous or wild fermentation, which would have been done 150 years ago in rum manufacture, due to maintaining quality control, Matt and Spencer felt that they were able replicate the rum as best as possible. The product they have created was a recipe that a Medford rum distillery like Lawrence and Sons Distillery could have used.

The name *GrandTen* came about when Matt was in business school, writing up the business plan that would become his distillery. He was trying to find a great Boston-sounding distillery name. He had a previous company called GrandTen Projects. For his business plan, he wrote in "GrandTen Distilling" as a placeholder until a final name could be chosen. When Spencer came on board, he loved the name and thought they should keep it.

More than just a tasting room, GrandTen offers a fantastic bar to enjoy a cocktail made with the fine spirits manufactured in-house. This company builds on the history of distilling in the Boston area but also thrives in the modern day, creating such tasty libations as Wire Works Gin, Medford Rum and many other fine spirits. GrandTen Distilling is located at 383 Dorchester Avenue in South Boston and can be found online at www.grandten.com. Although their tasting room and bar is located on a major road, finding the actual entrance can be tricky for first-time visitors. The large building that houses the distillery contains other businesses, including a Crossfit gym and a restaurant. Head to the left side of the building if facing it head-on, and the distillery entrance is located in what resembles an alley between two buildings, with another that is set back but bridges the two. The bar is perfect for kicking back and enjoying a drink. A bit of an adult playground, in addition to cocktails to sip, there is Nintendo Switch to play, as well as foosball and other games. Seating ranges from high tops and picnic-table style to couches and even a church pew.

NASHOBA VALLEY SPIRITS

Nashoba Valley Spirits has the distinction of being part of a larger craft spirit operation that includes the venerable Nashoba Valley Winery and Bolton Beer Works. Additionally, under the same banner is J's Restaurant, an award-winning bistro located at the farm. Nashoba Valley began as a pick-your-own farm and, decades later, has morphed into a one-stop destination for local wine, spirits and beer, as well as tasty food.

Where Nashoba Valley sits today was the Clemens Apple Orchard, a mainstay in the town of Bolton for many years. Eventually, after a period of decline, Jack Partridge bought the property in 1983. Partridge enjoyed making fruit wines, first out of his home and eventually out of a space in West Concord. Some of his recipes were actually ones that the Pilgrims used. He started his wine production at Damons Mills in West Concord. When he needed a larger facility, Upland Farm, as it was known then, fit the bill nicely. As a lover of American history, Jack planted over one hundred different kinds of apple trees on the property. Along with Jack, winemaker Larry Ames assisted in the operation.

Rich and Cindy Pelletier took over the operation in 1995. Richard Pelletier is the CEO and president of the company, and today it continues to be a family affair, with their son Justin as the chief operating officer. When

A taste of Nashoba Valley Spirits. *Courtesy of Justin Pelletier.*

the Pelletier family took over, they transitioned the winery into a destination unto itself. Included in this vision was the expansion of the winery by adding a restaurant and making it a venue for special events such as weddings and birthday parties. The Pelletiers brought Ames back into the fold to learn from his wine-making prowess; he would stay with the company until 2004.

One of the core values of the company is protecting farmland, agriculture and agritourism. They are a part of Massachusetts' Agricultural Preservation Restriction Program (APR). This program helps preserve farmland to make sure it is protected from development or construction.

Nashoba Valley Spirits is situated on a fifty-two-acre plot of land. About forty-five of those acres are covered with apple trees. The orchard is pick-your-own. Their line of hard cider as well as a few of the wines are from the apples grown on-site. In one season, there was a major surplus of apples, and the family had to decide what to do with it. This is how the distilling branch of Nashoba Valley began.

In 2003, Nashoba Valley was issued the first farm distillery license in Massachusetts. This means that they grow products on-site that then are turned into distilled products. For their vodka and gin lines, the base fruit or base ethanol is actually made from apples. (Nashoba Valley Spirits' gin was the first craft spirit this author ever tried.) The vodka and gin lines are completely gluten free. Just as their distillery line started with an excess of apples as a perfect way to make use of surplus fruit, today, any excess fruit is now used to make their vodka line.

Over the years, they have continued to develop their spirit line. Early on, they started making whiskey at a time when many local distilleries were not. In 2019, Nashoba Valley Spirits received a major investment with the acquisition of two Vendome stills. On a trip to Louisville, Kentucky, the Pelletiers went to Vendome Copper and Brass Works. The two customized pieces they purchased were a 250-gallon pot still with a vodka column and a continuous column still. From that expansion, Nashoba Valley Spirits has been able to hone its craft. The distillery has added many more products to the portfolio, including a bourbon line. Currently, their best-selling spirit is Northern Comfort. This is apple brandy aged for three to five years in a retired wine cask or bourbon barrel. After aging, Massachusetts-made maple syrup is blended into the brandy, as well as orange peel from a Massachusetts botanical company.

The bourbon line, which was recently rolled out, is made from three types of American-grown corn, along with American rye, wheat and traditional barley.

One spirit that Nashoba Valley releases that is harder to find in New England is an agave spirit that not many regional distilleries have thus far produced. It is similar to tequila, but tequila can be produced only in the Jalisco region of Mexico and four other areas of the country. Tequila is most closely associated with Jalisco. This makes the spirit like champagne, which can only be grown in that region of France. Nashoba Valley's agave spirit is made with 100 percent blue agave. This was one of the first products that ran through their pot still. Nashoba Valley also offers a white rum and a five-year aged rum that was stored in retired bourbon barrels or wine casks. They also make a few different cordials. One of their most popular flavored brandies is called Silk. This is a blend of peach brandy and peach wine. Similar is Elephant Heart, made from plum wine and plum brandy. Foggy Bottom is what Justin calls a "New England classic." This is made from oak-aged apple brandy, cranberry apple wine and mulling spices. This is seasonally released to widespread acclaim each November, just as the weather is turning chilly. Clearly, there is a spirit for every palate at Nashoba Valley.

Papa's Bourbon Whiskey. *Courtesy of Justin Pelletier.*

Currently, the tasting room at Nashoba Valley is located at the wine shop. During the COVID shutdown, the distillery was producing more hand sanitizer than spirits. Afterward, similar to so many businesses throughout the country, Nashoba Valley faced staffing shortages. In the near future, the plan is to open the distillery to the public for tours that include a tasting. This tour will give an overview of the equipment used and will allow customers to taste the full line of spirits offered by Nashoba Valley.

Also at Nashoba Valley is J's Restaurant, a much-lauded restaurant that has earned rave reviews from publications far and wide. It opened in 1998 in the circa 1920s farmhouse on the property. The complete operation at Nashoba Valley is a model of successful agritourism. Starting as a pick-your-own apple orchard, through the foray into wine making, followed by brewing and spirits, Nashoba Valley creates the idea of the farm as a tourist destination. Moreover, it takes fruit grown on-site and transforms it into a fresh product that is literally ripe for consumption. Couple that with J's Restaurant, a fine-dining bistro located in a beautiful historic home. The menu features seasonal fare. Past menu items have included salmon, scallops and tacos. Think butternut squash soup in the fall or a Statler chicken in the summer. While enjoying a glass of wine or a cocktail, take a jaunt through the garden to see the fruit ripe on the vine. Dining is available on the patio during the warmer months. The whole dining and drinking experience at Nashoba Valley is unforgettable. The restaurant is named after Justin and Jesse, sons of the Pelletiers. It earned the accolade of being among the best winery restaurants in the United States in 2019.

The orchard, still in touch with its roots, offers pick-your-own apples, peaches and nectarines in season. The Nashoba Valley complex is located at 100 Wattaquadock Hill Road in Bolton. Find them online at www.nashobaspirits.com.

PRIVATEER RUM

Following a tradition of rum distilling that began six generations ago, Andrew Cabot, founder and owner of Ipswich's Privateer Rum, takes his craft seriously. Andrew and his team use the best ingredients available to create the finest rum. With the name *Privateer*, the company is built on the maritime history of the region and has the same drive that the privateers who helped turn the tide of war during the American Revolution had for the United States to achieve independence.

Privateer specializes in rum, as it is all they make, with the exception of their gin. But even their gin is made from molasses. Rum is a spirit that has a certain stigma about it. Unlike defined styles such as bourbon or tequila, the taste of rum runs a wider gamut. For the last twenty-some years, rum has been waiting for its "moment," which has yet to arrive. Privateer relishes the challenge of rum manufacture and exceeds expectations of what rum is. We will learn about the distilling processes used at Privateer, the distribution process and the history behind the brand.

Step into the Privateer distillery, with its eye-catching tasting room adorned with a boat-shaped bar top and display shelves for its spirits that

A mojito made with Privateer's White Rum. *Photo by Reagan Byrne.*

resemble bookshelves lining an impressive library. Look into the distillery itself, listen to the popping sound of barrels breathing while aging the spirit inside and smell the sweetness of the rum being aged in new American oak. The distillery is located deep in an industrial park in the North Shore town of Ipswich. From the outside, the building looks like just another warehouse, but the interior is anything but. It is located at 11 Brady Road. Although the tasting room is not open to the public now, curbside pickup is available. Keep an eye out for special events to which the public is invited.

Privateer employs a hybrid still that is excellent for use in a craft distillery, given its versatility. Although Privateer focuses on rum, a hybrid still for many craft distilleries is able to provide the flexibility to distill a variety of spirits, such as gin, brandy and whiskey, all in the same still. For a distillery that makes many varied products, the hybrid still is the best way to go. Privateer uses their still to make six hundred barrels a year, classifying them as a medium-size distillery. Privateer focuses on rum, since that is where Andrew saw a weakness in the beverage industry. For years, rum has been deemed the "next thing" in the alcohol world. Be it 2019, 2009 or 1999, reports for years have mentioned this spirit as the next "it" beverage. Unlike other spirits, rum can be quite variable in taste, which leads consumers into a complex situation where they are unsure of the taste expectation. This is different from tasting a spirit such as bourbon or scotch, where there is knowledge of what the spirit will taste like. Rum's variability makes it a hard spirit to pinpoint. Privateer has been featured at tasting events worldwide, even in such faraway locales as Paris. Andrew shares a story of an event in Paris. At first, the attendees would say they did not drink rum, but halfway through the day, the line for Privateer was three or four people deep, and Andrew had trouble keeping up pouring his rum.

Although the Caribbean is often thought of in terms of rum making, actually, the weather in coastal Massachusetts is perfect for making the spirit. Climes such as those in the American South are too warm. In Ipswich, the sugarcane used for rum making can be harvested only four months a year and produces rum for nine or ten months. But the four distinct seasons in New England allow the perfect climate for barrel aging. The flavor results from the rum being aged in barrels made of new American oak. This wood brings a natural sweetness and vanilla essence into the product. Using the barrels in the climate of New England is beneficial, as it allows the barrels to breathe. The process of aging through the seasons allows for the contraction and expansion of the barrels, and this affects the spirit inside.

With rum uncharted for many consumers, Privateer offers a bridge to the drink. Using familiar flavors imparted through the spirit while barreled in white oak, the consumer may be inclined to partake in this rum journey through the familiarity of the taste. For Privateer, distributing to twenty states and seven countries, their consumers are on the national and international level. The appeal of rum is certainly not only for the community at large but also for rum lovers worldwide. As true champions of rum, Privateer sees its success as not only for the brand but also for rum on the whole. With rums such as their Barrel Proof Navy Yard and New England Reserve Rum, Privateer is breaking down past connotations of what rum tastes like. For much of the rum market, the primary category is spiced. This means that flavor is added to the rum. This rum has certainly never seen the inside of a barrel. Privateer is showcasing the true taste of rum. For example, the vanilla is directly from the new American oak; it does not have added vanilla flavor. The distillery uses no artificial ingredients, such as those used to create spiced, sweetened or flavored rum. The share of rum on the market that is flavored and/or sweetened is above 90 percent. Thus the expectation of many consumers of rum as a sweet concoction. This is certainly not authentic rum.

Andrew has personal connections to rum, as his family has a legacy of privateering. Six generations ago, the Cabot brothers, including Andrew Cabot, his namesake, were proponents of privateering. The Cabots owned over thirty privateering ships as well as Cabot Wharf in Beverly. On the wharf was a rum distillery (although colonial rum was certainly not enjoyed for its taste). Andrew was a millionaire in his day, and his home, built in 1783, is now the Beverly Town Hall. The Cabots were Massachusetts's second-wealthiest family. A personal connection to rum helped Andrew decide on it as his spirit of choice. With the dawning of the Revolutionary War, rum became less important and privateering more so. So Andrew Cabot sold the wharf and the distillery to focus on the fleet of privateering vessels.

Privateers acted like a civilian navy and were an integral part of the American victory in the War for Independence. Congress gave the green light for these sailors to interfere with the merchant fleet of England, interrupt shipping lines and even attack or capture enemy ships. Over 2,000 privateering craft employed between 55,000 and 70,000 men on these vessels. This led to the capture of 16 warships and 2,980 British merchant vessels during the American Revolution. Not only did the privateers help America turn the tide of war, but privateering was also a lucrative, albeit dangerous, business. Even though their main target was merchant ships, these were heavily guarded by cannons to prevent piracy, which ran rampant on the high seas. This added another level of perilousness to this endeavor. Altogether, roughly £50 million were awarded to American privateers of the high seas for capturing, attacking or plundering the British fleet, naval or merchant. Boats of all kinds were refitted from existing vessels, including cargo and merchant ships, to become privateering craft. The word *privateer* comes from the private ownership of the boats. This patriotic endeavor brought wealth to men like the Cabots of Beverly. Next door to Beverly, Salem was also a center for privateering. Pivateers also assisted greatly in the War of 1812, which saw the British patrol the high seas around the coast of New England. During this war, roughly 150 privateering boats from Massachusetts alone helped the American cause. Even later, during the Civil War, the Confederacy used privateering boats, but in the end this did not sway the outcome of the war in their favor.

Privateer began as a company in 2010, with its first release a year later. Andrew's background is in the technology field, and he even spent a year in the midst of his career teaching grade school in Boston. To begin his business, Andrew brought in a consultant from West Virginia with a background in whiskey. He also went out West to learn to operate a still, followed by a few weeks in the Caribbean to learn the process of distilling rum. While in the Caribbean, Andrew found that the best rum was not sent for overseas consumption but instead kept in the desk drawer of the distiller, which lent inspiration to the Distiller's Drawer specialty series of rum, which highlights extraordinary batches from Privateer. When investigating rum, Andrew was surprised to find that the top of the market was open. Much of the rum on the market was bottom shelf. It was enticing to him to try to make a high-quality rum. The first barrels bought were of new American oak. Starting out, an influence on Andrew was bourbon, which, although popular, did not have the same buzz as it does today. He was also influenced by brandies and French spirits. Even through the early days of Privateer, Andrew was able to set a house standard for their product. Through the years, Privateer has been able to improve its product through aging, practice and simply more knowledge. With rum as the only revenue stream of Privateer, they knew they had to make the product excellent. Unlike some distilleries, which offer a smorgasbord of different spirits, Privateer, with only one focus, knew its product had to be good.

Andrew relates that the first batches they made were fine, but he is embarrassed about the products they were putting out as recently as four years ago. Each year, his rum gets better and better. "We become insignificant the day we don't try and get better," he shared. Although consistency is a quality that the consumer looks for in a product, for a new craft distillery, staying consistent with the original would be a misstep. Instead, Privateer has kept honing its craft, with quality as a key to success. "We had to accept a pivot foot to always get better without completely abandoning what we have as our house style," explains Andrew.

As far as his favorite style, Andrew is biased toward those rums that are aged in new American oak barrels. At around two and a half years, the barrel-aging process makes the spirit take on new qualities, similar to what happens when aging an American straight whiskey. It continues to be reinvigorated as the aging process continues to four years, six years and so on.

One way that Privateer has been able to thrive has been through rum clubs. Most of the rum clubs (as of 2023) are less than four years old. For instance, the Florida Rum Society was started during COVID. Rum clubs help educate the consumer about rum and have become the foundation of the market. With Privateer distributing so widely, clubs help to get them into the glasses of rum-lovers worldwide. It is a different setup than a distillery with only local distribution. The idea of liquor clubs is so influential that major suppliers are actually catering directly to the clubs. Another concept that is thriving currently is the ownership of private barrels, which began with whiskey but has migrated to other barrel-aged spirits, such as rum.

Among the states where Privateer distributes is Tennessee. This state was targeted, since it is the heart of whiskey country. Privateer has pursued the true flavor profile of the American spirit, and even though it is rum, they

Step inside Privateer's tasting room. *Photo by author.*

have been able to thrive in the whiskey-dominated region. At the same time, Privateer has left its European market salivating for more. Andrew Cabot and Privateer have been able to take the true New England spirit of rum and create a product that is based on history and is utterly delicious. For more information, visit www.privateerrum.com.

RYAN & WOOD DISTILLERIES

Synonymous with Gloucester is Ryan & Wood Distilleries. The North Shore town has become part of the public consciousness due to its ties to the sea. This is underscored in books of seagoing endeavors such as Sebastian Junger's *The Perfect Storm* (later a movie). The small working-class coastal city is at the juncture of industry and tourism. Embodying this region, Ryan & Wood bills itself as "the Spirit of Cape Ann."

Ryan & Wood began in 2006 as a collaboration between Bob Ryan and his nephew David Wood. Ryan's background was in the seafood industry. As he relates, he "had no idea of the process." He was looking at starting a business that would be half steeped in manufacturing and half in tourism. Ironically, the idea for a distillery came to him while waiting for a haircut. He read an article about craft distilling in the *Wall Street Journal*, a newspaper randomly left out for customers to read. Initially, David was only partially involved, as he was a lawyer by day, but soon he became fully invested in it.

It was around this time that Gloucester was starting to reinvent itself from blue-collar fishing town to vacation destination. The seafood industry is an important one in the city, with brands including Gorton's, North Atlantic Fish and Ocean Crest. Bob wanted to show the seafood industry that other businesses could thrive there as well. For instance, the Parco family of Ocean Crest seafood had diversified and began the organic fertilizer company Neptune's Harvest.

By a stroke of luck, Bob found out that Bill Owens, president of the American Distilling Institute, would be visiting New England to check in on the handful of members of his organization at that time. Bob called Bill and offered to chauffeur him around New England. They visited four states, Massachusetts, New Hampshire, Vermont and Maine, on their three-day tour. Through the distillery visits, Bob was able to learn much about craft distilling. He approached his nephew David with the idea. After

From left, Doug and Bob Ryan and David Wood of Ryan & Wood Distilleries. *Photo by Kendra Dott's Double Exposure.*

further research and a business plan, "Suddenly our six-hundred-liter hybrid Holstein Still was delivered," laughs Bob.

Ryan & Wood is a family affair. Bob, sixty-eight at the time of writing, reflected on his career, "If I were a younger man, I'd be interested in conquering the world, but for now, Massachusetts will do fine." He added: "If someone else wants to take the helm, let me know. It has been an interesting and exciting ride." It is a true mom-and-pop business, as Bob and David started it with Bob's wife, Kathy, the proclaimed "queen of spirit tasting." She gives the verdict on what spirits hit the shelves. Through the years, Bob also enjoyed coaching Little League baseball. His son Doug is also part of the fold and works as a distiller (his full-time job is as a lawyer). David tragically passed away in 2014, but his spirit lives on through the company.

Beginning in 2006, Ryan & Wood was at the forefront of the craft distillery movement. Heck, that was even before a craft brewery could practically be found in every town. They started actual distilling in 2007, with vodka and gin first. The customer base at that time had a very basic knowledge of craft spirits, compared with the more in-depth appreciation of craft cocktails today. The average cocktail drinker at the distillery's inception was reaching for a vodka-based drink, often a variation of the martini. (Think Choco-tini, Espresso Martini or Appletini.) The Beauport Vodka was an immediate hit (and is still the biggest seller). Asked what his favorite drink is currently, Bob gladly shares that it is their Old Tom Gin, which is their Knockabout Cask Aged Gin, mixed with a little diet ginger beer. He calls it his "candy." In the portfolio of Ryan & Wood currently are three whiskeys: a straight rye, a wheat whiskey and a single malt; the Folly Cove rum; the Knockabout Gin and the cask reserve version of it; and the Beauport Vodka. Their whiskeys have also helped put them on the map. They still distill, bottle and sell a variety of hand sanitizers as well.

For the rum, Ryan & Wood uses an open fermenting system whose method is from Michael Delevante, a rum guru whose storied career includes being the head distiller at Jamaica's Appleton Estate, known for their rum. Delevante came out to Gloucester to teach Bob aspects of rum distillation and also told Bob to purchase a dairy chiller. He also recommended an idea to Bob that would forever influence his rum production. With the open fermentation process, marsh yeast from the Great Marsh, which runs from northeastern Massachusetts to southern New Hampshire, is able to infect the fermenting spirit. Michael recommended that Bob use this marsh yeast. A layer of carbon dioxide is formed on top, which keeps any insects away.

Gloucester itself has become more of a tourist destination since the inception of Ryan & Wood. The seaside town has been featured in a slew of television shows and movies, resulting in heightened popularity. In addition to the aforementioned *The Perfect Storm*, Gloucester's place in films goes as far back as 1937's *Captains Courageous* and to *CODA*, released in 2022, as well as the ever-popular reality television series *Wicked Tuna*. For tourists, Ryan & Wood is just one item in the tool belt of attractions that Gloucester has to offer, from gorgeous beaches, including Wingaersheek and Good Harbor, to the quirky but stunning Hammond Castle. There is also a variety of fantastic restaurants, as well as a vibrant downtown and artists' community. And there is the intriguing Dogtown and the seaside gem of a state park, Halibut Point. As the city has morphed, touches of upscale lifestyle seem to have infringed on the working-class community, but the blend of the two has resulted in a more vibrant town. Gloucester is a seaside community, and the beach and the sea are the main draws for tourists. On a rainy day, though, combine a trip to Ryan & Wood with visits to the quirky Hammond Castle and Cape Ann Museum.

The tragedy that inspired *The Perfect Storm* book and movie is one Gloucester event that Ryan & Wood will not be capitalizing on. Bob elaborates: "Being from 'Glousta,' there is a responsibility that goes with it. I could not think of tracking the advantages of tragic events such as marketing 'Perfect Storm' cocktails. I knew, worked with, played ball with, and drank with a couple of members of that crew. How could I face the families while profiteering from that event? It seems the whole town is of that mindset. And by the way, we have these tragic events often. As Gloucester lives, unfortunately, more often than anyone would like, it dies with the sea."

During the uncertain days of the pandemic, Ryan & Wood turned to making hand sanitizer. The Food and Drug Administration and the TTB permitted distilleries to produce sanitizer. As the spirits were not selling at this time, the excess gin was redistilled into hand sanitizer. Bob likens them to minutemen helping in time of need.

A tour of the distillery shows patrons where all of the action happens, from the mash tun to fermentation tanks to the still. The fermentation tanks have unique historical tie-ins to the names. One is the "Thomas E. Lannon," named after the schooner that takes seafarers around Gloucester Harbor on a pleasure cruise. The *Thomas E. Lannon* took its maiden voyage in 1997 and was built by the Ellis family, which operates it today. The name is in reference to Tom Ellis's grandfather, a fisherman out of Gloucester in the early twentieth century. Another tank is named "Adventure," for the schooner

Spirits aging at Ryan & Wood. *Photo by author.*

Adventure. This boat was built at the Essex Shipyard (like the *Lannon*) and was known as a highliner, as it was a very lucrative fishing vessel. It first launched in 1926 and still sails for pleasure today. Other tanks are named for the schooner *Ardelle*, another boat built in Essex, and the *Phyllis A.*, Gloucester's oldest fishing vessel, constructed in 1925.

The pride that Ryan & Wood showcases for their hometown is not just in "spirit" but also tangibly. Their labels feature local sites, including the image of the sea captain from the Fisherman's Memorial, nautical maps of the region and a schooner. Fun fact: Bob's grandfather, who was also a Gloucester policeman, acted secretly as security for rumrunners from Canada during Prohibition. This fact came to light when Bob was applying for his distillery license and the TTB caught up with him, inquiring about this fact.

For a taste of Gloucester, go beyond Gorton's and head to Ryan & Wood. Ryan & Wood Distilleries offers tours (and a tasting) at 10:00 a.m. and 1:00 p.m. every day from Monday through Saturday. Visit them at 15 Great Republic Drive in Gloucester and online at www.ryanandwood.com.

SHORT PATH DISTILLERY

At Short Path Distillery in Everett, it is all about using the finest ingredients to create their wide breadth of spirits. From gin to whiskey to even triple sec, it is hard to find a spirit that Short Path does not make. Not only do they pride themselves on high-quality ingredients, but they also make it a point to use as many locally sourced products as possible, hence the name "Short Path"—the ingredients take the shortest path from the farm to the mash tun.

Short Path was founded in 2015 by friends Zachary Robinson, Jackson Hewlett and Matt Kurtzman. As Zack relates, Short Path was "all founded on a love of scotch." In February 2012, the trio started a scotch club, where folks would get together, throw in $50, buy expensive scotch and drink it. The thought process was that if someone buys a $150 bottle of scotch, it sits there like furniture and isn't drunk. The club, by making less of a financial commitment, gave an excuse for the group to actually drink the scotch. Over time, the club became a monthly event.

One night, Matt joked, "Wouldn't it be cool if we did this ourselves?," as in making their own spirits. Zack's background is in organic chemistry, and at that time he was working for a pharmaceutical company. Distilling was part of his job at the lab. Granted, it wasn't alcohol, but he felt that his skill set there could translate well to distilling spirits. "It's just separating water and alcohol!"

From that initial thought, the trio set out to do research about opening a distillery. This eventually led to a business plan. The plan led to fundraising, which culminated with opening their own distillery. The whole process

The Moorish-style still at Short Path Distillery. *Photo by author.*

evolved organically from the initial idea without the establishment of a master plan from the start. Jackson by trade is a geotechnical engineer; Matt's background is in business.

Short Path was opened to the public in June 2015 after moving into the building the previous October. Before the distillery moved in, the building was basically a shell that had to be stripped down to the brass tacks. There was a fire in the previous incarnation of the building, a factory. A close look in the tasting room today reveals scarring from the fire. The building, erected in 1886, had always been used as a factory, most recently for Rubber Rite Rollers.

On the liquor side, scotch is what fueled the trio's distillery dream in the first place, with the goal of creating a New England Single Malt whiskey. Zack's favorite three spirits include this whiskey. The second of his favorites is the flagship gin, which was the first spirit they made successfully. Zack thinks that gin makes the best cocktails and is such a fun spirit to make. Clearly, he enjoys making gin—at the current time, Short Path offers seven varieties. Each gin is different from the others, but all are under the banner of gin. The third of his favorites is his apple brandy. The inspiration for this was a trip he made to Normandy, France, in 2010. He ended up in a distillery located inside a seventeenth-century chateau where they make Calvados, a French apple-based brandy that he fell in love with. From there, given the number of apple orchards in New England, his goal was to make a New England Calvados.

Along the way, the story of creating the series of gin has taken twists and turns. The Summer Gin is made with wild Maine blueberries. (Maine is Zack's home state.) The whole blueberries are soaked in the gin, causing them to absorb some of the alcohol. They crush the alcohol-infused berries to squeeze out the juice. These are put in the whiskey barrels for a year and then sweetened with honey from the bees that pollinate the very same blueberry fields. The final product is a sweet herbal blueberry liqueur. This was a happy accident.

The top-selling spirit is the triple sec. Zack laughs, "I started out to make whiskey, gin, and apple brandy but will be best known for my triple sec!" Short Path was the first distillery to have a bar. The law changed shortly before Short Path opened to allow distilleries to have bars. Other distilleries open at the time did not have a bar as part of their business plan, but a bar was added to the plan for Short Path. When it opened, only gin and rum were available, since other spirits had to be aged, which limits the number of cocktails that can be served. Zack made triple sec to increase the number of cocktails. The intention was for it not to be sold but to be kept in the well of the bar. Customers came in and really loved it. They asked if they could buy it. This was another happy accident. Zack figured it would only be sold at the distillery, but accounts started asking about it, and soon it was available in stores and bars. They started to wholesale it. It became the fastest-growing spirit in their vast portfolio, and in 2021, it became the biggest seller. I joked that Short Path should use the tagline "Making Everett more cosmopolitan."

Tasting the triple sec is a vastly different experience from the syrupy sweet triple sec usually served. This is made with real oranges with organic orange peel, whereas the large brands use extracts. Bitter and navel oranges are used in the recipe. Navel oranges have a candied orange flavor, while the bitter orange is richer, with a true orange flavor when distilled. The balance between the two allows it to have depth but still have the candied orange nose on the first sip. It contains just 10 percent sugar by weight, much less than the typical 25 percent found in most triple secs. Popular cocktails include Skinny Margaritas with the triple sec, since the sugar content is much lower. Also, the bartenders are then able to modify the sweetness of the drink by how much of it is used in the drink. If someone wants a sweeter drink, the amount of Short Path's triple sec can be doubled, but that is still less sugar than in a typical brand. The ABV is 20 percent, more than most others in the genre.

Short Path's seasonal gins also have an interesting backstory. Having four seasonal flavors was not initially in the plans. There were the Summer and Winter gins when Short Path was developing gin flavors. Initially, the Winter Gin was served as a one-off test batch called Gin Number 14. The drink was going to be called "Rosemary Gin," as rosemary was the primary botanical. The government, which has to approve all labels, said that the drink could not be called Rosemary Gin without a reason being given. Zack wanted to call the Summer Gin "Blueberry Gin," since there are blueberries in it. The government also said no to that name. Zack pushed back, asking why the decision was made. The reason was that "Blueberry Gin" would confuse the customer; they would think there was added blueberry flavor in it. Zack said that there is a blueberry flavor in it derived from actual blueberries. The term *blueberry* can only be used when an artificial blueberry flavor is used. Ironically, if Zack had called it "Blueberry-Flavored Gin," the name would have been approved. If a product hails itself as "Pineapple Rum," the pineapple used is simply a chemical concoction mimicking a pineapple flavor. Each distillery has to submit the recipes to the Alcohol and Tobacco Trade and Tax Bureau. The average recipe page for Short Path, since they use natural ingredients, is one-third to half a page, whereas the average recipe submission for liquor is thirteen pages. The larger companies fight hard not to put the ingredients on the label for alcohol, blinding the customer to what they are actually drinking. For instance, a mass-produced gin may not have actual juniper in it, just juniper flavor compounds chemically created to add to base alcohol. Short

Path has stayed away from the Ready to Drink (RTD) canned cocktails, since it is hard to use actual flavorings in them. Orange flavoring can be from actual oranges, but it would be tough for Short Path to replicate their use of actual whole oranges in creating canned cocktails. Natural products would have to be pasteurized, which leads to less consistency in the taste.

Once the Summer and Winter gins were created, both names approved by the government, Short Path needed to make Spring and Autumn gins to round out the seasons. The seasonality has worked well for the gin but has not been successful with other spirits as of this time, since most customers view spirits as timeless and not seasonally appropriate, unlike beer or even coffee, whose industries often use seasonal themes in their beverages.

Their whiskey, a New England single malt, is made with all products found in the Northeast. This is an example of local products that have taken the "shortest path" from their place of origin to the distillery. The name is also a pun, since "short-path distillation" is a scientific name for distilling done in a pot still. They made the decision to use local grain in their whiskey and chose Valley Malt from Hadley, Massachusetts, as their source. The idea is to use local grain instead of Midwest grain to make a truly local product. Similar to wine, where the terroir of where the grape is grown affects the flavor of the wine, this is true for grain as well. From the beginning, Short Path wanted to use only local grain. When making whiskey, they use 100 percent local grain.

In 2020, the Northeast Grainshed Alliance held a major event at Trillium Brewing Company, with about two hundred participants. The event consisted of talks, with the main message about using local grains. Zack became heavily involved in the alliance. It is a collection of brewers, malters, bakers, distillers and farmers. Other brands involved include One Mighty Mill, a flour company from Lynn, Massachusetts; Trillium; and many other breweries. They are all companies across the Northeast. The group showcases the benefits of using locally grown grain. One benefit is a smaller carbon footprint, since shipping from the Midwest uses an immense amount of fossil fuels as compared with sourcing in the Northeast. Also, if there is a breakdown in a supply chain, locally grown product allows New England to feed itself instead of relying on the transportation of goods from halfway across the country. It recently took eighteen months for ordered bottles to arrive, compared with the weekly delivery of local grain. The reliability of the "shortest path" is just one of the many benefits.

Being a farmer is difficult enough. Grain is a rotational crop. This means it can complement the growth of typical crops such as vegetables or tobacco. In normal circumstances, the field would remain fallow in alternate years, which means the field is not producing any kind of income. If farmers can grow grain instead, this replenishes nutrients in the soil and creates income in a year when there would have been none. With the natural nutrients being added, farmers are able to spend less money on fertilizer and there is thus less runoff of fertilizer into streams, lakes and rivers, which is better for the environment. Growing wheat also breaks the pest cycle. If a farmer is growing only potatoes, they have to use increased amounts of pesticides to combat the potato beetles. If the grain is grown during the in-between year, the potato bugs will not eat the grain and will die off. When the pests that eat grain start to pop up, the field then is used for potatoes again, swapping back and forth, which combats the insect problem. In short, the growth of local grain helps the environment, provides more income to farmers and saves them money. For the companies involved, a major benefit includes consistency, with the grain being delivered without issue when needed. Another plus is the stabilization of prices, since shipping from the Midwest is more expensive due to fuel and delivery costs. Additionally, a symbiotic relationship has been created between the farmers and those who use the grain. The farmers take the utmost care, and the producers such as brewers, bakers and distillers take pride in where the grain comes from. These farms working directly with the producer can grow a specific grain varietal that has been requested, since they are working through the whole process from seed to finished whiskey. The malter will malt the grain to specifications outlined by Short Path. The process is very collaborative.

Last summer, a new member was added to the Grainshed. Morrill Farm, a dairy farm that had an excess of fields being used for food stock for cows, decided to switch over to growing grains for breweries and distilleries. As people are drinking less cow's milk and opting for alternatives such as oat and almond milk, a smaller herd of cows was needed. This farm's owners invited brewers and distillers to the farm in Concord, New Hampshire. They showed the visitors the farm and even treated them to a tractor ride. From there, Zack and the farmer came up with an idea of a "single year, single farm, single whiskey," so the entire production is based on one grain from one farm. In 2021, Short Path used only rye and barley from Morrill Farm. This initiative has proved to be beneficial for all parties and makes sense both environmentally and business-wise. (And it's a cool story, to boot!) The customer wins, because they get great whiskey. Zack is now on the board of directors for the Grainshed.

Short Path is the only distillery in Massachusetts that uses 100 percent locally grown grain. Others use local, but not entirely. Local is defined as grain that has been grown within three hundred miles of the distillery. The region is all of New England and eastern New York, with a small amount also coming from northern New Jersey, all the same bioregion. With the states in the Northeast relatively small, a bioregion comprises climates and terrain that are similar. Midwest grains cannot be grown in New England due to the completely different weather. In the past, to start growing grains, farmers had to go to seed banks to find heirloom varietals, since grain had not been grown in New England for many years. During the first year of the new process, the grain is grown in a ten-by-ten-foot plot and then is harvested. The following year, it expands to a one-acre plot, and finally, after year four, commercial farm size is reached. Farmers had to take the risk in this endeavor without knowing that it would be successful. Currently, it is proven that these grain varietals have worked well for brewing and distilling. Not only are they locally grown, but they also are Northeast-specific varietals of barley, wheat and rye.

Short Path uses a direct fire copper pot still, which is made in Portugal in the traditional Al-Ambiq style. There are no moving parts to the still, so a lot of flavor comes through on the pot still. Only about ten distilleries in the United States use direct fire, including three in the Northeast, one in New York and one in Maine. The still itself is Moorish in design from Portuguese manufacturer Al-Ambiq, which has been around since 1837, and would look at home in *Aladdin*. Short Path's still produces apple brandy that has a pronounced apple pie flavor. For distilleries that use a traditional steam-jacketed still, the apple brandy's flavor has a crisp taste. The whiskey also has a cooked, bready taste due to the still. The pot stills are run slowly, creating a lighter finished product that is still full of flavor. Short Path's whiskey is stored in fresh American white oak barrels. They work with Adirondack Barrel Cooperage in Remsen, New York. It is a small company that can work with Short Path for their specifications, including using local wood. The finished whiskey is close to a Speyside scotch. Speyside is a northeastern region of Scotland that includes whiskey distilleries such as Glenfiddich and Aberlour. Currently, it takes about three weeks from grain to barrel to make the whiskey before it begins aging in the barrel.

A major goal of Grainshed is to bring awareness of how much grain is needed for various products. This is called the Square Foot Project. One can of beer uses about four square feet of grain, one bottle of Short Path whiskey needs sixty-eight square feet and one cocktail uses four square feet. This shows how many farms are needed. If all local farms are sold off and turned into housing, the ability to make local products such as whiskey, beer and bread will be increasingly difficult. With a six-pack of beer, using commodity grains, a farmer gets four cents, but using local grains, a farmer gets forty cents.

Zack's passion has been for creating things. When working for the pharmaceutical company, his role was new drug discovery, creating new medicine. This has carried over with the vast number of spirits found at Short Path. There are twenty-seven spirits in the repertoire, including vermouth, ouzo and amaro, which most craft distilleries are not making.

Each spirit is represented by a different bird. The wood thrush is depicted on the apple brandy labels, the peregrine falcon on the peated whiskey and the turkey vulture on the rye whiskey. The spirits from Short Path are truly spectacular. They are easy to drink by themselves, with plenty of flavor, but are also perfect in a cocktail. Find Short Path at 71 Kelvin Street in Everett or online at www.shortpathdistillery.com.

SOUTH HOLLOW SPIRITS

Located close to the tip of Cape Cod in Truro, South Hollow Spirits is worth the drive for its array of excellent spirits presented in a sensational setting. South Hollow Spirits is located at Truro Vineyards at 11 Shore Road in North Truro.

Arriving at the complex, what visitors notice first is the beautiful setting. The Federal-style home dates from 1813 and is currently used as the store of the vineyard and distillery. There are tables scattered throughout the lawn for drinking and noshing from nearby restaurant Blackfish's Crash Pad food truck, which serves absolutely delicious bites. Other buildings on the property include the distillery itself and a building that houses a barrel room and winery. Adjacent to this is a patio with more tables and rows and rows of grapes growing in the sandy soil of Cape Cod.

Truro Vineyard began operation in 1992 by New York State residents Kathy Grogow and Judy Weimer, with the Roberts family taking over in 2007. Owner Dave Roberts had a storied career in the beverage industry, which included twenty years as CEO of United Liquors, an alcohol wholesaler and distributor. On retirement, he wanted to pursue wine making himself. Today, the vineyard and distillery are a family affair, with the owner's wife, Kathy, and their children in charge. The head distiller is Dave Roberts Jr., and the CFO is his daughter Kristen. The co-owners are the two Daves and Kristen, while Bill Melody is the assistant distiller.

Left: Assistant distiller Bill Melody gives a tour. *Photo by author*.

Right: Welcome to the Truro Vineyards and South Hollow Spirits complex! *Photo by author*.

The property has been a working farm since the 1800s. One of the most striking features in the yard is the colossal Chinese mulberry tree. This is a remnant of a failed silkworm farm that was attempted on the property by Captain Atkins Hughes in the 1830s. Unfortunately for him, the silkworms died within the first year. Hughes eventually passed the farm into the hands of Abigail, his daughter, and her husband, Michael Rich. They used the property as a working farm and sold milk and grain. The vineyard and environs sit on roughly four acres. In addition to the grapes grown here, ten other vintners around the country grow grapes for Truro.

The visitor experience at Truro Vineyards / South Hollow Spirits can be catered to one's desires. A tour, a tasting, a meal, a visit to the store— all of these are options for the visit. For the full South Hollow experience, my recommendation is a tour followed by a sampler flight of spirits. South Hollow Spirits employs a beautiful Vendome still, which is the showcase of the quintessentially New England–looking, white-washed distillery building. During the tour, listen to the description of the processes of fermentation and distilling. It is informational and entertaining, which is the perfect balance— it even holds the attention of kids, who are often in tow, as Cape Cod is the tourist mecca of New England, especially in the summer. Detailing the spirit-making process, the terms *heads, hearts* and *tails* are discussed on the tour. Of the distiller's cuts of the spirit, the heads are even passed around so that visitors can smell the intensity of this nail polish–esque liquid. This always results in a few scrunched-up faces of those who sniff it.

Botanicals used for gin or other spirits are literally dunked into the alcohol like a giant tea bag steeped into a cup of tea. The barrel room is stunning, with murals of Cape Cod adorning the walls. The experience is reminiscent of a Tuscan farmhouse. The distillery is in the process of building its own space for its barrels, separate from the wine barrels. The current barrel room has an amazing fragrance. The barrels South Hollow uses are made of American, French or Hungarian oak. Through the doors of the barrel room, look at the bottling line, where 350 cases of wine can be bottled in a six-hour period.

South Hollow has a line of exquisite and award-winning spirits. The rum line is called "20 Boat." It has an interesting backstory. The name refers to the rumrunning days of Prohibition, when one outlaw was pursued after he and nine others were arrested in Dorchester Bay near Boston. After posting bail, he escaped via boat with rum in tow. For his getaway, he headed toward Cape Cod and, in the process, eluded a fleet of twenty boats, with police and U.S. Coast Guard in pursuit. The smuggler safely made his escape and disappeared into Provincetown. The distillery produces a four-and-a-half-year and a six-year aged amber rum, as well as a white unaged amber and spiced rum. Other spirits include gin, which is actually made from their white rum and is called "Dry Line." Try the rosé gin, which is 65 percent gin and 35 percent rosé wine. They also offer an eighteen-month barrel-aged gin. (South Hollow offers Dry Line gin ready-to-drink cocktails, too.) Their whiskey is highly lauded and is named after the family's dogs, including Ruby, Lucy and Otis. This is a robust rye, aged for five years. South Hollow also distills two different amaros,

If Cape Cod resembles a flexed arm, Truro is the wrist. The Cape becomes incredibly narrow, so Cape Cod Bay and the Atlantic Ocean are separated by only the small swath of land that is Truro. What this means for growing grapes is that the soil is sandy, which is actually good for growing the fruit. Among the varietals of grapes grown on-site are Chardonnay, Cabernet Franc and Merlot. These grapes are harvested typically in October, which is about eight to twelve weeks behind the grape-growing regions of California. Truro runs a community harvest for picking the grapes. This has become a fun event, with participants taking home a bottle of wine. Walking among the grapevines, one notices netting. This netting is used to keep birds away from the vineyard. Not only does the netting cover the top, but it is also extended to the ground, as wild turkeys enjoy pecking at the lower-hanging fruit.

Tasting the spirits at South Hollow is not similar to doing so at other distilleries. For one, given the wine component, there is a different approach. Customers sit at a table and can choose from a cocktail using the South Hollow Spirits, a glass of wine or a flight of wine or spirits. The spirit tasting involves whatever is available at that time, and four tastings come in a flight. A fun part of both the spirit and wine tasting is that the glass is yours to keep. I always enjoy a sampler, since it lets me try the company's products, be it spirits, cheese or jam. It also lets me decide what I would like to take home in bottle form. (The ability to try a delicious cocktail is tempting, too, to see what exquisite creation can be concocted from it.) The flight also allows tasting of spirits that may be off one's radar. For instance, maybe you are familiar with base spirits such as vodka, rum and whiskey, but an amaro is a spirit that is new to you. The flight lets you sample this taste, which may be your new favorite spirit or perhaps one you will stay away from. But that is the joy of sampling. The amaro is an herbal liquor with a bitter taste, which on a personal note I enjoy, but it can be too adventurous or simply not enjoyable to some. South Hollow offers not only an amaro but also a variation of it known as Amaro Cioccolate. It's an amaro made with cocoa nibs. Tasting this in the flight is a fun way to experience an altogether new taste. The word *amaro* actually means "bitter" in Italian, and the Amaro Cioccolate is both bitter and sweet, as the chocolate adds an extra layer of sweetness to the bitter taste. Although this is fun to try, I typically opt for South Hollow's regular amaro, as this flavor profile is a winner to me, whether as an aperitif, an after-dinner drink or part of a cocktail such as a Negroni. Another favorite to sample is the rosé gin, as the flavors of the wine and the gin blend seamlessly with one another.

South Hollow Spirits and Truro Vineyards is a perfect non-beach diversion while visiting Cape Cod. Stop in for a tasting, a tour, a glass of wine or a cocktail while soaking in the splendid setting. With its consistently strong reputation, Truro Vineyards has been a must-visit for decades. South Hollow Spirits is yet another reason to book a visit to this slice of paradise near the tip of the Cape. Grab yourself an exquisite bite from the Crash Pad, such as a juicy hamburger or perfectly crafted tacos, and order a flight of South Hollow Spirits, a finely executed signature cocktail or a glass of their award-winning wine. Imbibing while basking in the warm Cape Cod sun and cooled by the sea breeze, relaxing in the midst of this beautiful property, you just may never want to leave! Visit them online at www. southhollowspirits.com.

TRIPLE EIGHT DISTILLERY

Nantucket's Triple Eight Distillery was the first distillery founded in Massachusetts in the modern era. It is also one of the most well known, for good reason, as they have been earning accolades and medals longer than most others have been around. Triple Eight's owners are Randy and Wendy Hudson and Dan and Melissa Long. Triple Eight is owned and operated as part of a family of craft libations, including the well-regarded and -loved Cisco Brewers and Nantucket Vineyard.

Actually, those who would like to visit Triple Eight's tasting area on Bartlett Farm Road in Nantucket may be surprised to find more than just spirits. Also on-site is the vineyard and the brewery, presenting a trio of craft options for the consumer. During the summer, Nantucket's busiest season, expect a come-as-you-are party atmosphere, often accompanied by live music and food options, with patrons sitting at picnic tables. Although Nantucket is known for its premium price tags, visiting the complex is welcoming for everyone, whether you have $5 million in your bank account or $5.

Given its location at 5 Bartlett Farm Road, it is not within easy walking distance to downtown Nantucket, where the commercial ferries disembark passengers. Thankfully, Cisco runs a shuttle van on Wednesdays to Sundays to help customers access the complex.

Nantucket Vineyards was the first of the three operations, beginning in 1981, with owners Mellissa and Dean Long. Due to the difficulty of growing grapes in Nantucket, the grapes they initially used were imported. A few years later, they were able to grow their own on their farm. Randy and Wendy began to live above the winery and helped out at the vineyard. In the early 1990s, Cisco Brewers followed. The final endeavor between the two couples became operational in 2000 as Triple Eight Distillery. Triple Eight is named after the well that gives water to the distillery, number 888.

Triple Eight distills a wide variety of spirits, among them vodka, rum and whiskey. Randy and Bryan Jennings are the head distillers. The first spirit distilled was vodka, due to the excellent water found on the island. They offer a line of fruit-based vodkas, including blueberry, with fruit imported from Maine, which turns the typically clear liquid a robust purple. The Blue was voted twice in five years the best flavored vodka in America at the World Vodka Awards. The cranberry vodka is made with cranberries from Nantucket and Cape Cod and is red in hue. The orange vodka is created with orange zest. The vanilla vodka is made with vanilla from New Guinea and Madagascar. The raspberry vodka includes fruit imported from Oregon, and their organic vodka won best in the category by the American Distilling Institute. Triple Eight uses real fruit, never flavorings or chemical compounds.

Sipping cocktails in the summer sun at their craft libation destination is a popular pastime. Certain mixed drinks including the Cranberry Vodka Soda and the Blueberry Vodka Soda have become bestsellers. More recently, Triple Eight has canned these, turning any backyard into a miniature version of their home base. The Vodka Cran and Vodka Blue have proved to be just as popular (and tasty) as their cocktail counterparts at the distillery. Other flavors include tequila and lime and grapefruit. These are gluten free and are easy to drink at 4.44 percent. They are very refreshing, and the fruit taste permeates, but not in an overpowering way.

Given Nantucket's seaside location, storms are bound to hit the island. But there are a few storms on the island that are welcome. These are in the form of spirits, including the Nor'easter Bourbon, which is made elsewhere but barreled on Nantucket. Gale Force Gin is made with nine botanicals, and the Hurricane Rum is aged somewhere between four and twelve years. The spirit that has brought Triple Eight numerous accolades has been the Notch Whiskey (think Not-Scotch). There is a twelve- and a fifteen-year-old, the latter aged in sherry casks. It was named Best Single Malt Whiskey in the country in 2015 and over the years has claimed this title on multiple occasions, most recently in 2022. It has been a Double Gold Winner at the San Francisco World Spirits Competition and has earned the distinction of "platinum" after winning three golds. Notch was called the "world's best small batch single malt whiskey" at the 2022 Whiskey Magazine Awards in London.

While visiting Triple Eight, make sure to try a cocktail. Ingredients such as mint, chamomile, raspberries, cucumber, kale, garlic and peppercorns are grown on-site and are used to make tasty creations. Located far away? Their products are available for sale in twelve states.

For a taste of the island life, make sure to get your hands on a bottle of Triple Eight's premium spirits, including their blueberry and cranberry vodkas, or their Notch single malt. Try a canned cocktail from your local package store, or if possible, get to the number-one craft libation destination at 5 Bartlett Farm Road in Nantucket for a fun-filled afternoon with Triple Eight, Cisco Brewers and Nantucket Vineyard. Visit them online at www.tripleeightdistillery.com.

WORKING MAN DISTILLERS

Aging spirits at Working Man Distillers. *Photo by author.*

Working Man Distillers celebrates the blue-collar, hardworking individuals who help make the community function. Owned and operated by the husband-and-wife team of John and Kelly Lendall, the distillery is housed in a former industrial space in North Attleborough. The story of Working Man is also that of John and Kelly's relationship, as they are intertwined.

Ironically, initially for John, whiskey was not his drink of choice. Kelly helped him realize his love of the spirit. On one of their first dates, Kelly brought over a bottle of whiskey. John did not feel like beer that night, and Kelly's preferred libation was wine. She picked up a bottle of Angel's Envy whiskey. From then on, the couple became interested in whiskey. Eventually, they learned to nose it, learned about the flavor profiles and experimented with imbibing in different ways—over ice and neat. As John explains, referring to whiskey, "We fell in love with it!" It was something that they could enjoy together as a couple. They found that, after going out to dinner, they would come home for a glass of whiskey as a nightcap. John also found that, unlike beer, which often filled him up quickly or added to the fullness of a meal, the whiskey did not have the same effect. From enjoying a glass of whiskey after dinner, John and Kelly moved on to pairing whiskey with food at dinner.

Their initial foray into whiskey tasting took them on the road. The couple traveled up and down the East Coast, venturing to different distilleries. One distillery that John desperately wanted to visit was at Mount Vernon, George Washington's estate. James Anderson was Washington's farm manager and encouraged the former president to begin whiskey making and set up a distillery on the property. Reading a book about Washington furthered John's curiosity about making spirits. In 1799, the year that Washington died, his distillery produced roughly eleven thousand gallons of whiskey and was one of the largest manufacturers of the spirit in the young country. The Mount Vernon Distillery is still producing whiskey and can be visited today.

After exploring the world of distilleries, Kelly bought John a home distilling kit. There was one caveat: Kelly held the kit hostage until John offered her a marriage proposal. Soon enough, their kitchen was turned into a science project distilling "essential oils."

Shawn Hogenmiller, who was the director of operations at Green Mountain Distillers in Morristown, Vermont, helped guide John in the process of opening up a distillery. Kara Larson and Cathy Plourde of Rhode Island Spirits in Pawtucket, Rhode Island, also helped guide the Lendalls. Although Pawtucket is out of state, it is located right next to Attleboro. All three of these individuals were extremely helpful to John and Kelly. John thought they might try to talk him out of opening his own distillery, but all three mentors were very encouraging. They also outlined other perks of owning a distillery, which, in addition to the creative, marketing and interpersonal aspects of the job, include being one's own boss and being able to make one's own hours. John and Kelly also consulted Boston Harbor Distillery about whiskey making.

As a newer distillery, opening its doors in 2020, Working Man had to figure out what was best for their business plan. As whiskey is their favorite spirit, John and Kelly wanted to make sure that it was featured prominently. The problem with whiskey is that it takes years to age. To combat that, they decided to initially outsource whiskey that they would redistill in-house. Working Man also mashes and distills in-house on a smaller scale. Bringing it in from the outside is also financially less burdensome, since buying the finished product by itself is much more cost-efficient than obtaining the grain and other ingredients used to make the initial batches. Although a shipment of grain costs roughly $400 and a new barrel of outsourced whiskey alone is $600, there are many additional expenses in the process of going from grain to glass, bringing the cost far above the $600 whiskey barrel. Many distilleries employ this method of using a starter spirit before it is redistilled in their facility. Among the more popular companies to buy from is MGP (Midwest Grain Products) from Indiana. Whiskeys, including the previously mentioned Angel's Envy, Bulleit Rye and Batcher's Bourbon from Litchfield (Connecticut) Distillery, all started from MGP. Distilleries use a whiskey originating at MGP and then blend and redistill it.

The tasting room at Working Man is inviting and eye-catching. The decor focuses on the "working man" theme, with items including fire helmets, first responder memorabilia and mixed martial arts (MMA) photographs by Kelly. Kelly is a professional photographer who for years took photos of MMA bouts. John is a plumber by trade and comes from a blue-collar family on the North Shore. The plumbing background came in handy when setting up the distillery, since he was able to do so much of the plumbing himself. The distillery is located out of the public view in the back of their space, with access to the parking lot with a garage bay. Working Man often hosts events, including a variety of food truck pop-ups. These feature area gourmet restaurants, including Burgundian, a restaurant in Attleboro that specializes in street food of all kinds. Burgundian's food truck sells their delicious Liege-style waffles at the distillery. Certainly not limited to food, Working Man has even hosted blood drives

John, who is the head distiller at Working Man Distillers, started with pot distilling, basically making moonshine. He then had to learn the whole process of distillation. Although not originally from Attleboro, John enjoys the area very much, as it is full of history and only a quick drive to Providence, Rhode Island. Kelly and John also enjoy working with each other, as they are not only married but also best friends. Their relationship is conducive to the work setting, since they do not always agree on every aspect and often have to compromise. As John explains: "I don't want someone to yes me to death. If it is not good, I want to know. If you see something that I could do better, let me know." Kelly provides the creative criticism and feedback needed to balance their operation. Their dynamic is perfect for the working environment.

Their Blue Collar Bourbon is popular, especially since many folks come in and say that they only drink bourbon. It is surprising to many customers that bourbon does not have to be made in Kentucky. As champagne comes only from the Champagne region of France and tequila from certain parts of Mexico, many people assume that bourbon has to be made in Bourbon County, Kentucky. At Working Man Distillers, they also encourage expanding one's palate. Even if someone is a bourbon drinker exclusively, John and Kelly encourage visitors to try the rye whiskey. In most cases, they thoroughly enjoy Deadlift, their signature rye whiskey.

The distillery has even made absinthe, a spirit that most New England distilleries have not tried. For the absinthe, Working Man gets their grapes from La Cantina Winery in nearby Franklin. Only five gallons were made in the initial run. People loved it, and it sold out very quickly. Absinthe is not only rare but is also hard to get government approval for. Working Man had to submit the label six times before approval. The ingredients in the absinthe include chocolate mint, lemon balm, fennel, star anise, wormwood and alfalfa leaf. The number of ingredients made it hard to get the recipe approved. Even the inclusion of chocolate mint threw off the TTB, which didn't realize that chocolate mint is actually a plant and not mint chocolate candy or flavoring. The color of the drink was not a deep green, different from what many think absinthe should look like.

Working Man purchases its yeast through Dr. Patrick Heist's Ferm Solutions. Heist teaches the fermentation course at Moonshine University in Louisville, Kentucky. Heist also owns Wilderness Trail Distillery. For barrels, they most often turn to Adirondack Cooperage in Upstate New York.

The distillery formed an LLC in 2019 and signed a lease on its distillery space at 42 Commonwealth Avenue, Unit 4, in North Attleborough a year later. The tasting room opened in the late summer / early autumn of 2020. At first, John and Kelly thought that the distillery would offer only tastings but eventually decided otherwise. Working Man received its pouring permit approval in December 2020 and introduced a cocktail menu in their tasting room. The Lendalls felt it would make more sense for them not to put their initial effort into distribution but instead into the tasting room, where customers could try their spirits as part of a cocktail. The tasting room is at the heart of their business. The cocktail appeal reaches a whole different audience than customers who solely want to buy a bottle to take home for creating cocktails or drinking neat. For instance, many customers who come in for a cocktail say that they do not like whiskey, but once they try it in a cocktail, it leaves them with a changed mind. This way, the whiskey connoisseur can enjoy it neat or on the rocks, while the novice drinker may enjoy it as part of a favorite cocktail such as an Old Fashioned.

With the company and tasting room steadily moving ahead, John and Kelly started creating a draft cocktail system. This way, popular cocktails are at the ready through draft lines in the tasting room. This is a quicker way for the customer to receive a drink. Once poured, it just needs to be garnished and then is in the customer's waiting hands. A customer favorite is their Black Manhattan on draft. A Black Manhattan replaces the typical sweet vermouth with an amaro. With a Farmer's Distillery License, Working Man can only sell what they make as far as alcohol goes. They take pride in their cocktails, knowing that at a distillery, especially one that does not serve food, the cocktails have to be dynamite to keep customers coming back. Although they do not have a kitchen, they serve cheese boards, skewers and finger wraps, and they invite food trucks to share their goodies or encourage patrons to visit local restaurants for food. John's go-to cocktail is an Old Fashioned for a whiskey drink. He also enjoys gin martinis as well as a gin and tonic.

Working Man Distillers has been able to fill a much-needed void in the region southwest of Boston. Although not far from either Boston or Providence, North Attleborough is not full of bars and restaurants offering specialty cocktails, and this is where Working Man steps in. Instead of a basic mundane Manhattan of whiskey, simple syrup, an orange slice and a maraschino cherry, at this distillery's barroom, they muddle the orange with half a teaspoon of sugar with the rye whiskey and then muddle it again with bitters, stir it nicely and pour it over ice. This takes a bit more time, but steps such as the muddling release oils and flavors from the peel that the cocktail would otherwise lack.

In the tasting room, visuals also help pull customers toward a cocktail. They may see someone with an intriguing creation and inquire what it is and end up purchasing one themselves. One such cocktail is the Moonshine Pina Colada, which has become a customer favorite. Patrons also enjoy seeing the bartenders take those extra steps to make their drink extra delicious. This also becomes a roundabout way of advertisement, as customers often take pictures or video of the process that will most certainly be added to their Instagram page or story. Friends or followers then see it, are intrigued and may find their own way to Working Man Distillers to taste it for themselves. Unlike many independent companies that spend much money on search engine placement on Google, billboards or print advertisements, Working Man Distillers' advertising is organic. By tags on social media and followers of their accounts, the word gets spread. And by following their Facebook page, customers are able to see what special events are lined up for the coming week, such as food options, live music, drink specialties and new releases. Working Man even has a loyalty program that already topped five hundred people in less than two years.

For a tasty cocktail creation southwest of Boston, make sure to swing by Working Man Distillers. Visit them at 42 Commonwealth Avenue (Unit 4) in North Attleborough and online at www.workingmandistillers.com

PART IV

RELATED FIELDS

MR. BOSTON OFFICIAL BARTENDER'S GUIDE

Of all alcohol brands, new and old, the one that has the strongest relation to the city of Boston has to be the Old Mr. Boston brand. Yes, rum as a specific spirit has the most historic connotation, but in name, it has to be the Old Mr. Boston brand. This brand was a fixture in the city between 1933 and 1986. As a distillery, it offered a full range of spirits, including cordials and liqueurs, brandy, gin, vodka, rum and bourbon. The distillery was started by Bostonians Hyman C. Berkowitz and Irwin "Red" Benjamin in 1933. After a few acquisitions, the company was purchased by Louisiana's Sazerac in 2009. Over the years, the brand changed from Old Mr. Boston to Mr. Boston to, finally, Boston. Under the current Sazerac ownership, it has been revived once again as Mr. Boston. Although Mr. Boston is no longer distilled in the city or even in Massachusetts, with the purchase of a property in Lewiston, Maine, under the Boston Brands moniker, Mr. Boston is once again made in New England.

More than just a brand of spirits, Old Mr. Boston was also known for its recipe book, *Old Mr. Boston's Official Bartender's Guide*. Beginning with its first publication in 1935, the guide could be found in the back pocket of many a bartender and behind the bar at most drinking establishments. The guide's thoroughly detailed cocktail recipes became a lifesaver for bartenders of all kinds. After Prohibition was repealed in December 1933, there was an advent of cocktail collections such as this guide.

"The Cocktail Guru," Jonathan Pogash, author of *Mr. Boston Official Bartender's Guide*. *Photo by @ CaseyMcMurray*.

"Sirs—May we now present to you Old Mr. Boston in permanent form, we know you are going to like him," began the book. Although Mr. Boston was a fictional gentleman, his knowledge was real. Initially, Mr. Boston was depicted as a portly middle-aged fellow, Victorian in appearance, with top hat and pronounced sideburns. The modern-day Mr. Boston keeps the hat but is a much younger man. The books were edited by Leo Cotton, who worked for the brand. Initially a hobby, updating and revising the editions of the guide was a passion for Cotton. The first edition "was compiled and edited by four old-time Boston bartenders," according to the guide. Cotton revised and updated the guidebook through its forty-ninth anniversary in 1970, when he retired.

The latest in-print version of the book was completely updated and redone by Jonathan Pogash, one of the country's foremost experts on cocktails. He was nicknamed "The Cocktail Guru," and that is also the name of his company, which offers a wide range of cocktail services, including classes, special events and consulting services. Pogash has been featured on a variety of television and radio programs and in publications.

Jonathan grew up in the industry. His dad, Jeffrey Pogash, worked at Moet Hennessy USA. Prior to that, he studied wine and the art of wine tasting in Paris. For many years, Jeffrey was the representative from the United States for CIVA, an organization based out of the Alsace region of France for those in the wine industry. Clearly, Jonathan was raised in the alcohol industry. Jeffrey, now retired from Moet Hennessy, also works for The Cocktail Guru and is an author in his own right. His most recent book is 2011's *Bloody Mary*.

Jonathan rose through the ranks of the bartending industry. His initial foray into the field was as a barback at the Russian Tea Room in Midtown Manhattan, a historic and iconic one-hundred-year-old restaurant. He transitioned from barback to bartender to helping open restaurants. Pogash is from New Jersey and spent much of his career in New York City.

Pogash moved from New York to the Massachusetts hometown of his wife. During this hectic time in his life, between moving and being an expectant father, Wiley and Sons, the publishers of the *Mr. Boston's Official Bartender's Guide*, approached him about revising a new edition of the book. He co-edited the book with Rick Rodgers, a chef and cookbook author. Pogash was recommended for the new edition by the previous edition's editors, Anthony Giglio and Jim Meehan.

Once on board, Pogash only had a few months to revamp this book. His first question for his publishers was, "Can I rip this book apart?" What Pogash and Rodgers did was completely overhaul the book. They had to partake in thorough recipe testing and needed to eliminate from this edition recipes that simply could not be modernized. Not wanting to rely on their own devices, they were able to tap into the knowledge of bartenders around the world. They also wanted to make sure that for certain recipes in the book, the bartenders who created them were credited. The introductions had to be beefed up, and photos had to be added. For Pogash, this guide became more like a full-time job than a side project.

The book was released in 2011 as the 2012 edition. He was able to organize a book tour in major cities across the country, including Los Angeles, New York and Boston. He toured with his dad, who had recently released *Bloody Mary*. The father-and-son book tour was a hit, and liquor brands supported the tour. As far as research for the guide, Pogash was lucky that his dad, forever in the industry, had quite the library of cocktail literature spanning centuries. In addition, his dad had in his collection all of the Mr. Boston guides from the initial edition in the mid-1930s to the present. Jonathan relates that even during his time at the Russian Tea Room, the book was behind the bar. The bartenders would take a quick peek if they were unsure of a requested cocktail. This book has been the safety net for decades of bartenders.

As the "little red book" has been a barroom staple for generations, Pogash did his part to update it for the modern era. Unfortunately for traditional book lovers, modernity has caught up with it more than expected. Sazerac has taken the classic title and digitized it. Handy for the twenty-first-century bartender or armchair mixologist, the website lists the anthology of drinks by recipe at www.mrbostondrinks.com. The browser can also view the cocktails by year, from the 1935 edition to the present, which makes it a pretty amazing resource. Currently, twelve editions are available for perusal on the website. The collection includes books that Mr. Boston himself would enjoy. This sophisticated collection is the antithesis of the many online drink libraries that, in addition to barroom staples, sometimes contain disgusting "cocktails" often submitted by college students that exist solely as a vessel for drunkenness. The Mr. Boston website contains 1,500 cocktail recipes. With the digitization of twelve different editions of the guide, 10,540 historic recipes are available online. For those who enjoy the tangibility of a printed book, past editions can still be found in some bookstores, used bookstores and online.

For us in Boston, the former Old Mr. Boston distillery can be viewed from the outside today at 1010 Massachusetts Avenue in the Roxbury neighborhood. The building is owned by the city and houses offices such as the Boston Public Health Commission. Seeing it today, it is remarkable how large this operation was. Although the Mr. Boston brand left Beantown almost forty years ago, with Jonathan Pogash's contribution to the legacy of the Mr. Boston guides, he has been able to put a bit of Massachusetts back into the Mr. Boston story.

For more information about The Cocktail Guru, visit Pogash's website at www.thecocktailguru.com. Visit the digitized *Mr. Boston's Official Bartender's Guide* at www.mrbostondrinks.com. The full line of Mr. Boston spirits from Amaretto to watermelon vodka with everything in between, from rum to gin to ready-to-drink cocktails, can be found in most major liquor stores.

IRENE TAN

Irene Tan is a Level 3 Whiskey Sommelier who has worked with distilleries far and wide as part of her consulting business, Whisky Mentors. A whiskey expert, although based in Connecticut, she has close ties to Boston Harbor Distillery and has worked with others, including Working Man Distillers, for events that she hosts. Additionally, in her store, Canterbury Liquors in Canterbury, Connecticut, she features products from distillers in Massachusetts, such as Boston Harbor and Bully Boy Distillers. As an avid barrel collector, she even has barrels of Boston Harbor's Putnam Rye in her possession.

Irene's whiskey passion started through wine. As she says, she had "too many bottles of wine in her basement." Too many is 1,200 to be exact. At that moment, she said to herself that she had better open a store. When asked if she is a collector, she laughs and replies, "No, I'm a wine drinker!" She partnered with the store Brooklyn Northeast Wine and Spirits, becoming co-owner. She handled the whiskey aspect of the store. Her love of whiskey took off from there.

Author Zack Lamothe and Irene Tan at Whisky Mentors. *Photo by Jim Wheeler.*

She was working in Franklin, Massachusetts, at the time (home of GlenPharmer Distillery) and attended every whiskey tasting she could, which amounted to a couple of times a week. During that first year, as she puts it, "I tasted way more whiskey than a person should." Her whiskey career is her retirement hobby. Her nine-to-five job was as a software consultant.

A few years later, around 2016–17, Irene saw the whiskey world really take off and decided to stay in this field, first and foremost because she loved it. Unlike folks who have been drinking whiskey their whole lives, Irene's maiden voyage occurred in 2014. For her, it was not a single whiskey that ignited the flame. It happened gradually. She was also happy that, like wine, she could enjoy it with food.

As a Level 3 Whiskey Sommelier, Irene is a trained whiskey professional. With her impeccable palate, she is able to offer food pairings, whiskey advice and extensive overall knowledge. She was familiar with the levels of wine sommelier and was looking for something similar for whiskey. She found that in Austin, Texas, the Whisky Marketing School offered a program to become a whiskey sommelier. She loved the program. The inspiration that she felt on the campus was all-encompassing.

She does not have a favorite style of whiskey. Instead, it depends strictly on the day, the mood she's in, the company she is with and the food she is eating. She appreciates and understands what goes into making whiskey. Instead of deeming a whiskey good or bad, she believes it is subjective. If the style presented is something that someone does not like, it does not mean that it is bad whiskey. Instead, it may simply not be well-matched to the individual's palate.

One whiskey she recalls fondly is a Laphroaig 32 Year. She explains, "I didn't even want to taste it because it just smelled so good!" She nosed it for about thirty minutes before finally tasting it. Although bottles like the Laphroaig come with a hefty price tag, Irene believes that more than how expensive the bottle is, it is really about those who are enjoying the beverage with you. "It could be a $20 bottle or a $1,000 bottle, it's who you are sharing it with."

At Canterbury Liquors, Irene sells a phenomenal selection of whiskey. Additionally, in the room adjacent to the store is Whisky Mentors, which is lined with whiskey of all kinds. Although most bottles can be found next door, she also has barrels from all over the world.

The story of the development of Irene's whiskey collection is fascinating. For instance, she has purchased eighteen barrels from Garrison Brothers Distillery in Colorado. This brand had to grow on her. When she first tasted it in 2014, she felt that it was not quite there yet but knew it was a brand she had to follow. There was something there that called out to her. Soon after, she bought her first barrel, then two more. The distillery had blossomed into making a finely crafted product. She feels that with this distillery, she has evolved along with it. Similar to this is Kings County Distillery in Brooklyn, New York. When their product first came out, they were in small barrels and had a woody flavor to them. Fast-forward to the winter of 2020. She tasted their rye and thought it was excellent. She asked how many cases they had left in Connecticut and decided to take the whole bunch. Now this distillery is so well regarded that the first barrel from them sold out within a month. The next barrels she gets will be spoken for right away.

She buys barrels simply because "they taste so good to me!" Her barrel picks are not run of the mill. To her, there has to be something special, maybe a different variation or something else that makes it stand apart. Since starting in Canterbury, she has actually named every single one of her barrels, the first being "Irene's Winter Warmer." The barrel selection process is very personal. She has to like it enough that if no one wants to buy it she will enjoy the contents herself for the next three years. The intimate relationship that she creates with the barrel is what leads to her naming each of them. Typically, she names the barrel after tasting it in the morning, when her palate is really clean, a day or two after she has picked it. She tastes all of the nuances of the flavor before she names the barrel. Her customers actually know the barrel by the name she has given it rather than by the distillery.

As a frequent barrel customer, Irene is able to taste what barrel or barrels she would like before purchasing and actually rejects many. She prefers to travel to the distilleries to pick the barrels she wants. Distilleries will send samples, but she likes going to the source, even though it takes much longer. Her customers believe in the barrels that she picks. Although it may be a few dollars cheaper to purchase a bottle of the same spirit, her customers believe that her palate will choose a barrel that is worth the extra money. Irene's barrel picks now number in the triple digits! Sixty-seven barrels were purchased for the Canterbury store in the first two and a half years (including time when things were paused with the COVID-19 outbreak).

Some of the bottling she will do, but most often the distillery does the bottling. She has gone to Boston Harbor Distillery to bottle whiskey. In 2017, Rhonda Kallman, founder of Boston Harbor Distillery, called Irene out of the blue. As one female business owner to another, she wanted to know if Irene was interested in taking a trip to Boston to see what they had, in case she wanted to buy a barrel. Six barrels were pulled aside for Irene to taste. The first barrel she tasted was barrel number fifty-six, which she remembers fondly. On first smell, she knew that this was amazing. She told Rhonda to put her name on the barrel but to keep it for a year, since she did not think it was quite ready yet. It was a 95 percent rye and 5 percent two row malted barley. This barrel spoke to her, as it imparted so much flavor while aging only for a year and a half. Then, 364 days later, Rhonda delivered Irene's barrel with the bottles. That is how Irene's relationship with Boston Harbor got started. The second barrel she has from them, a 127.4 proof, she named "Stay Awhile." As she says, the reason for the name is twofold. "If someone pours you some and you like it, you'll want to stay awhile. And due to the high proof, after a few sips you should stick around for a while!"

All of Irene's barrels are cask strength, which means there is little or no dilution to the whiskey after its tenure inside the aging vessel. The only exceptions are the major distilleries, which do not allow it to be bought at cask strength, including Knob Creek, Elijah Craig and the Fighting 69th. Irene does keep it local when possible, which includes Bully Boy, as well as Whistle Pig and Mad River Distillers from Vermont. She adds, "People in the Northeast are making good whiskey and good spirits in general." Although whiskey is her specialty spirit, she also has a barrel-aged gin from Barr Hill in Montpelier, Vermont.

In addition to the rye, Irene has a barrel-aged version of Lawley's Gin from Boston Harbor Distillery. She went to the distillery and tweaked the botanical recipe a bit, adding some extra ginger and extra blood orange. The altered recipe could then be aged in her Elijah Craig barrel. She happily explains: "It's pretty damn good right now! I'm excited about it." Her barrel has notes of dark cherry, so she wanted the recipe to be altered to give it a Kentucky Mule flavor or that of a Negroni, which would come through with the extra fresh orange. Currently, she has been able to try it after it has been aged for around eight weeks, and it is already tasting fantastic.

Irene prefers to drink her whiskey neat. She understands that adding water will make the nose more pronounced but feels it loses the mouthfeel. Water will make the alcohol taste come through too strongly. If she adds anything to whiskey, it is when she is making a cocktail, such as a Manhattan, a personal favorite. In the cocktail format, the focus is no longer on the whiskey in its pure form but instead the whole meld of taste.

Although she herself does not distill, she does blend. She takes certain whiskey barrels and blends them to her liking. For instance, the barrels she has named "Sweet Hot Cocoa" and "Cinnamon Toast" work very well blended together. Irene will let customers taste the whiskeys by themselves and then blended together.

Visit Canterbury Liquors at 180 Westminster Road (Route 14) in Canterbury, Connecticut. To visit Irene at the adjacent Whisky Mentors, set up an appointment with her by message via Instagram or Facebook. On Facebook, there is actually an option to set up an appointment with her. The usual tasting lasts about half an hour to forty-five minutes. The conversation delves into the customer's palate preferences and understanding of what they would like to explore. Typically, around six to eight small tastes of whiskey are given. Irene enjoys teaching the customers about whiskey and trying to match what she thinks they will like. Irene taught English and physical education when she started on her career path and has come full circle, teaching customers about whiskey. Not only a teacher, she also learns from every conversation she has and focuses on building relationships with her customers. She also advocates for a responsible way to enjoy whiskey. It is not about getting drunk; instead, it is about experiencing it. Make sure to keep an eye out to see what work Irene is continuing to do with Boston Harbor Distillery as well as with Whisky Mentors.

ADIRONDACK BARREL COOPERAGE

Located in Remsen, a small town in Upstate New York, Adirondack Barrel Cooperage exemplifies a major component of the craft distillery process: the aging of spirits. Many of the Boston-area distilleries purchase their barrels from Adirondack Barrel Cooperage, including Working Man Distillers, Chattermark Distillers and Short Path Distillery. The cooperage is known for its barrels of the highest quality.

Adirondack Barrel Cooperage is owned by the husband-and-wife team of Joe and Kelly Blazosky. Joe's background is in carpentry. He owned his own construction company for about thirty years. He did almost every job in the construction industry, including building custom homes and restaurants, renovation, custom furniture and cabinetry. The reason why the couple landed in the barrel-making field was the barrel shortage of 2013. Distillers at the time were facing a crunch and were being given wait times of eighteen months to two years to receive their orders. Joe was looking to apply his carpentry skills in a new way or in a different industry. Joe and Kelly struck up a conversation with a local distiller and decided to make a foray into barrel making. The distiller told them that they had had to delay making any

Adirondack Barrel Cooperage and mascot. *Courtesy of Adirondack Barrel Cooperage.*

aged spirits and had to focus on making clear spirits as a result of the lack of necessary barrels.

Joe and Kelly spoke with other distilleries in New York State and on the East Coast. They asked the distilleries if they would be interested in working with them if the Blazoskys started a cooperage. The answer was a resounding "yes!" After doing research, the Blazoskys found that there was not a cooperage of any significant size in the Northeast at that time. Barrels were being imported from the South, Midwest and West Coast.

The heat is on! *Courtesy of Adirondack Barrel Cooperage.*

Distilleries were not the only businesses interested in the cooperage. Wineries and breweries also took notice. All of these businesses reacted positively when the Blazoskys were doing their market research before opening. This encouragement gave them the wherewithal to keep moving forward with their idea.

Kelly's background is in travel and tourism. She is the president of Oneida County Tourism. This is the region in central New York where they are located. The craft beverage industry is a huge movement and one that is very important for travel and tourism. Travelers and locals alike seek out food, beverage and culinary options. Adirondack Barrel Cooperage has been a good fit for Kelly.

The staves used in the barrel production are air-dried, not kiln-dried. This makes a significant difference in the flavor profile of the barrel, which then is imparted to the spirit inside. The raw staves are made from oak trees from Missouri and Minnesota. Without a mill on-site, the staves come in a blank raw state and are then processed at Adirondack Barrel Cooperage. In the future, the Blazoskys hope to continue their relationship with the current mills but would like to forge a partnership with a stave mill in New York as well to meet the growing demand for their barrels.

The following steps are done in-house. The barrels are raised by hand and then fire-bent. Fire bending is a process that only a few cooperages in the United States do. It is the traditional French method of barrel making. The barrel is placed over a fire cresset, which resembles an iron basket, and

Charring the barrels. *Photo by Max Kelly Photography.*

it is dampened with hot water. The heat makes the barrel bendable so that it can be closed. It is bent into the complete shape of the barrel by hand. The barrels are then toasted at a low temperature by hand before being charring or toasted further. Wineries may request extra toasting for their barrels, whereas distilleries typically desire charred barrels. The toasting adds an extra layer of depth to the flavor of the barrels.

The cooperage works with their customers to provide the desired specific product. Some ask for an extended hand-toast, which means the barrel will be toasted further than is typically done. Customers also set their char level. Standard levels of char are one, two, three and four. Some customers want those levels tweaked a bit based on the flavor profile they are looking to achieve from their spirit. At Adirondack, they are able to satisfy these needs. Each barrel is sanded, finished and pressure-tested for leaks, after which they are branded, wrapped and then shipped out. They are built when ordered, so it is not as though these barrels have been sitting out. They are made to order. They are fresh when shipped, and every order is built specifically for the customer.

The majority of Addirondack's customers, roughly 85 percent, are distilleries. Another 15 percent are wineries, and less than 1 percent are home winemakers or people purchasing barrels for fermenting food such as sauerkraut. One of their customers is the Connecticut-based soy sauce manufacturer Moromi, which makes small-batch soy sauce in the traditional Japanese style, fermented in barrels. With the utmost customer service, Joe talks with customers directly if they need a recipe changed or wish to discuss toast and char levels. Having a good relationship with a cooperage is essential to distillers, winemakers and anyone else who relies on barrel-aging for their product. Given its size, Adirondack Barrel Cooperage is able to maintain a strong relationship with all of its clients. The Blazoskys want to stay at a size where they can continue to forge this kind of partnership with their customers.

Luckily, at a time when COVID slowed businesses worldwide, the same effect did not happen to the cooperage. Most of their customers kept their orders in place. Addirondack was fortunate to continue to be able to operate, as cooperages were not shuttered. The industry was deemed essential. The largest COVID-related issue had to do with the shipping and transportation industries. Higher prices and a lack of transportation resources led to an increase in shipping costs.

For us Boston-area imbibers, the next time we are sipping a barrel-aged spirit such as Chattermark's bourbon, we should take a minute to reflect on the craftsmanship and skill used in making the barrels that the spirit was aged in. We should also consider how the oak is used and how the toasting and charring process affects the spirit itself. Cooperages and distilleries go hand in hand—more like spirit in barrel. You can't have one without the other.

Part V

Cocktail Recipes

ow it is time for a taste of the Boston-area distilleries. Here is a compilation of delicious cocktails from many of the region's fine craft distilleries. Try your hand at making them at your own home.

Bean
GlenPharmer Distillery

2 ounces Bean
1 ounce Irish Cream
½ ounce Pumpkin Spiced Simple Syrup

Prep: Add all ingredients to shaker filled with ice.
Shake vigorously. Strain into a martini coupe. Garnish with toasted pumpkin seeds.

Bhut
GlenPharmer Distillery

2 ounces Bhut ghost pepper vodka
1 ounce mango juice
1 ounce orange juice
¼ ounce Cilantro Simple Syrup

Prep: Mix all ingredients into shaker filled with ice.
Shake vigorously. Pour (do not strain) in highball glass. Garnish with fresh cilantro.

Blood Orange G&T
Short Path Distillery

2 ounces Short Path Distillery Gin
1 ounce blood orange juice
2 teaspoons Fever Tree Aromatic Tonic Topper

Add gin and blood orange juice to a Collins glass filled with ice. Top with Aromatic Tonic and stir to incorporate ingredients. Garnish with a blood orange slice.

Bog
GlenPharmer Distillery

2 ounces Bog
½ ounce blood orange juice
1 tablespoon cranberry sauce (whole berry)

Prep: Shake all ingredients with ice.
Pour into a rocks glass (do not strain). Top with fresh orange zest.

Brookdale Gin
GlenPharmer Distillery

2 ounces gin
1 ounce passion fruit puree
1 ounce sour mix
¼ ounce egg white
3 dashes plum bitters

Prep: Mix gin, passion fruit, sour mix and egg white into shaker with ice. Shake vigorously. Strain over fresh ice in highball glass. Add plum bitters to the egg white foamed top.

Charlestown Buck
Chattermark Distillers

1 muddled strawberry
1 ½ ounces bourbon
1 ounce lemon
½ ounce simple syrup
2 dashes aromatic bitters

Shaken, serve in a highball glass filled with ice. Topped with ginger beer.

Chocolate Mint Old Fashioned
Working Man Distillers

2 ounces Ten Mile River Rye
½ teaspoon sugar
1 orange rind
4 chocolate mint sprigs

Muddle all ingredients together until sugar is dissolved. Stir in ice and pour over a big rock. Garnish with orange rind, mint and a peninsula cocktail cherry.

Cranberry Mule
GlenPharmer Distillery

This is an elevated mule that will have you forgetting about Moscow. The key is GlenPharmer's Bog®, a wheat vodka infused with fresh, locally sourced cranberries.

2 ounces GlenPharmer Bog® Cranberry Vodka
½ ounce fresh lime juice
4 ounces ginger beer

Add all ingredients to copper mug (or glass) and top with ice and ginger beer. Garnish with mint, lime wheel and cranberries (or just a lime wheel).

Dark Tide
GlenPharmer Distillery

2 ounces Dark Tide
3 dashes Aromatic Bitters
1 Luxardo cherry
1 orange slice
1 sugar cube

Prep: In rocks glass, add sugar cube, orange and bitters and muddle. Add Dark Tide, stir. Add 1 large ice cube.

Deacon's House Negroni
Deacon Giles Distillery

In rocks glass:
1 ounce Juniper Point Dry Gin
1 ounce Amaro Diacono
1 ounce falernum
4–5 dashes orange bitters

Stir gently 15–20 times over ice. Strain into rocks glass. Serve neat or over a single large cube. Garnish with expressed lemon.

Dry Line Harvest Punch
South Hollow Spirits

2 ounces Dry Line Cape Cod Gin
2 ounces apple cider
1 ounce honey simple syrup*
½ ounce fresh lime juice
1 apple

Combine all ingredients in a shaker over ice. Shake well and strain over new ice into a Collins glass. Garnish with an apple slice.
*To make honey simple syrup: Combine equal parts water and honey in a small saucepan over low heat. Stir until mixture is combined and let cool before using in cocktail.

Good & Plenty
Short Path Distillery

1 ounce Short Path Distillery Ouzo
1 ounce Short Path Distillery Triple Sec
1 ounce orange juice
½ ounce grenadine

Add all ingredients into a shaker filled with ice and shake. Strain into a rocks glass and garnish with an orange slice.

Jamaican Me Crazy (Rum Old Fashioned)
Boston Harbor Distillery

2 ounces Lawley's Dark Rum
½ ounce maple syrup
2–3 dashes Jamaican-style bitters

Mix together and serve over ice.

Lavender Bee's Knees
GlenPharmer Distillery

This cocktail incorporates lavender syrup to create a beautiful presentation that also pairs perfectly with the eleven botanicals in GlenPharmer's Brookdale® Gin.

2 ounces GlenPharmer Distillery Brookdale® Gin
½ ounce honey
½ ounce fresh lemon juice
½ ounce lavender syrup

Add all ingredients except lavender to a shaker with ice. Shake and strain into martini or coupe glass. Drop in ½ ounce lavender syrup. Garnish with fresh honeycomb (or lemon wheel).

Liberty Tree Boston
AstraLuna Brands

50 milliliters Liberty Tree Boston Rum
25 milliliters sweet vermouth
2 dashes orange bitters
Orange twist
Maraschino cherry

Place ice in a cocktail shaker. Add rum, vermouth and bitters. Stir. Rub the orange peel around the rim of the cocktail glass. Strain the drink into the glass. Add 1–2 real maraschino cherries.

Nail Biter
Boston Harbor Distillery

1 ½ ounces Putnam Rye
1 ½ ounces Demon Seed Whiskey
1 ounce Fiery Ginger Syrup
½ ounce maple syrup

Shake, then strain into a coupe glass. Garnish with a Thai chili pepper.

Newmarket Martini
Bully Boy Distillers

1 ½ ounces espresso-infused Bully Boy Vodka
1 ½ ounces cold brew
½ ounce cardamom syrup

Add all in tin. Shake, then strain into coupe. Garnish with rose petals.

Nocino Manhattan
Chattermark Distillers

2 ounces rye
¼ ounce nocino
1 teaspoon cherry syrup
2 dashes aromatic bitters

Place cherry in coupe. Stir and pour.

Old Tommy B
Ryan & Wood Distilleries

2 ounces Knockabout Old Tom Gin
1 ½ ounces ginger ale
1 ounce lime juice
½ ounce simple syrup

Combine gin, lime juice and simple syrup in a shaker with ice. Strain into a rocks glass over ice. Pour ginger ale over and stir.

Painkiller
South Hollow Spirits

1 ½ ounces Twenty Boat Spiced Rum
Painkiller mix (see below)
1 dash fresh ground nutmeg
1 orange wedge

Painkiller mix
2 cans Coco Lopez

32 ounces orange juice
46 ounces pineapple juice

Privateer Daiquiri
Privateer Rum

2 ounces Privateer New England White Rum
1 ounce fresh lime juice
1 ounce simple syrup

Combine in a mixing glass, add ice and shake. Strain into a coupe glass.

Privateer Gin Negroni
Privateer Rum

1 ½ ounces Privateer "Tiki Inspired" Gin
¾ ounce Campari
¾ ounce sweet vermouth

Combine in a mixing glass, add ice and stir. Strain into a rocks glass filled with fresh ice and garnish with an orange twist.

Privateer Jet Pilot (Tiki Drink)
Privateer Rum

2 ounces Privateer New England Reserve Rum
½ ounce fresh lime juice
½ ounce fresh grapefruit juice
½ ounce falernum
½ ounce cinnamon syrup

6 drops absinthe
1 dash Angostura bitters

Combine in a mixing glass, add ice and give a short shake. Strain into a glass filled with crushed ice and garnish with mint sprig.

Privateer Mojito
Privateer Rum

2 ounces Privateer New England White Rum
1 ounce fresh lime juice
1 ounce simple syrup
8–10 mint leaves
½ cup soda water

Combine in a tall drinking glass over ice, mint first, and shake. Top with soda water and garnish with a mint sprig.

Privateer Palmetto (aka Rum Manhattan)
Privateer Rum

2¼ ounces Privateer New England Reserve Rum
¾ ounce sweet vermouth
1 dash Angostura bitters
1 orange twist
1 cherry

Combine in a mixing glass, add ice and stir. Strain into a coupe glass and garnish with an orange twist and cherry.

Privateer Queen's Share Swizzle
Privateer Rum

2 ounces Privateer Queen's Share Rum
1 ounce fresh lime juice
1 ounce simple syrup
8–10 mint leaves
2–3 mint sprigs
3–4 dashes Angostura bitters

Combine mint leaves and simple syrup and gently muddle. Add rum and lime juice, fill with crushed ice and swizzle. Garnish with Angostura bitters and mint sprigs.

Privateer Rum Old Fashioned
Privateer Rum

2 ounces Privateer Navy Yard Rum
½ ounce simple syrup
2 dashes Angostura bitters
2 dashes orange bitters

Combine in a mixing glass, add ice and stir. Strain into a double old-fashioned glass filled with fresh ice and garnish with an orange twist.

Raising Arizona
Deacon Giles Distillery

2 ounces Green Tea Vodka (see below)
¾ ounce Runny Honey (see below)
1–2 drops ginseng extract (optional)
6 ounces soda water

Build in Collins glass. Top with soda water.
Garnish: Matcha powder

Green Tea Vodka

1 750-milliliter bottle Yankee Ingenuity Vodka
2 high-quality green tea bags (Deacon Giles prefers Twinings)

Remove tags and strings from tea bags. Stuff tea bags into vodka bottle. Allow to sit and infuse for 24 hours. No need to remove the bags, just use when ready.

Runny Honey

½ cup wildflower honey (or good-quality honey of choice)
½ cup hot water

Combine honey and hot water. Stir until honey is dissolved. Keep refrigerated when not in use. Discard after 2 weeks.

Shimmering Cape
South Hollow Spirits

2 ounces Twenty Boat Spiced Rum
1 ounce ginger liqueur
Splash of cranberry juice
½ ounce passion fruit puree
Crushed red chili pepper flakes
1 piece candied ginger

Combine Twenty Boat Spiced Rum, ginger liqueur, cranberry juice, passion fruit puree and chili pepper flakes in a shaker with ice. Shake well. Serve up in a chilled martini glass. Garnish with candied ginger.

Spiced Rum
GlenPharmer Distillery

2 ounces spiced rum
2½ ounces hot steeped apple cider
1 dollop of fresh whipped cream
1 dash cinnamon
1 star anise

Topped with fresh-whipped cream, cinnamon and star anise.

Velnias Sour
Dirty Water Distillery

1 ½ ounces Velnias Spiced Honey Liqueur
1 ounce lemon juice
½ ounce simple syrup

Shake all ingredients with ice. Strain into glass with new ice. Garnish with lemon peel. Enjoy.

Watermelon Crush
Short Path Distillery

2 ounces Short Path Distillery Gin
1 ounce watermelon juice
¾ ounce lemon
¾ ounce simple syrup
1 spring mint leaves

Add gin, watermelon, lemon and simple syrup to a shaker filled with ice. Place mint in the palm of your hand and slap it with your other hand to release its oils. Add slapped mint into the shaker and shake. Strain into a rocks glass filled with ice. Garnish with a mint bouquet.

White Hot
Chattermark Distillers

1 ½ ounces white rye
¾ ounce lemon juice
¾ ounce jalapeño simple syrup

Shake, then serve in coupe glass.

Woodward
Bully Boy Distillers

2 ounces Bully Boy American Straight Whiskey
½ ounce cinnamon syrup
½ ounce amaro
3 dashes Peychaud's Bitters
3 dashes Regan's Orange Bitters

Build all in tin. Stir. Pour into smoked Nick and Nora glass.

Epilogue

For me, one of the most rewarding aspects of writing is learning about the topic I'm investigating. Taking a subject, whether it be booze or boos (in reference to folklore, which I've studied extensively), it's digging into the research that brings me joy. This title was by far one of, if not the most, fun I have had in writing a book. First of all, my prior expertise in the area was more about enjoying a tasty cocktail rather than understanding the science behind distilling. Not only did I walk away having learned much more about how to make alcohol than I ever guessed I would, but I was also able to meet some truly fantastic people along the way. There was not one distillery that I visited that did not welcome me with open arms. When drinking spirits from the Boston area, know that these libations are crafted with love and care by truly excellent individuals. I hope you have enjoyed this trip through the distilleries of Boston, taken in a little history and science along the way and learned how to make a damn good cocktail using local spirits. Cheers!

BIBLIOGRAPHY

Beverly Historical Society. "Privateer Trail: Beverly's Revolutionary Era Maritime History," March 2017. www.historicbeverly.net.

Bouchard, Fred. "Truro Vineyards." *Massachusetts Beverage Business*, December 1, 2008. https://beveragebusiness.com.

Brooks, Laken. "Why Did Women Stop Dominating the Beer Industry?" *Smithsonian Magazine*, March 8, 2021. https://www.smithsonianmag.com.

Brown, Nell Porter. "Grow, Make, Eat, and Imbibe." *Harvard Magazine: Issue January–February 2014*, December 16, 2013. https://www.harvardmagazine.com.

Bushard, Brian. "Triple Eight Blueberry Vodka Named Best in America." *Inquirer and Mirror*, February 24, 2022.

———. "Triple Eight Notches Another Win." *The Inquirer and Mirror*, March 31, 2022.

Cheever, Reverend George B. *The Dream: Or The True History of Deacon Giles's Distillery.* New York: Thomas Hamilton, 1859.

Cronin, Andrea. "Three Centuries of Molasses in Massachusetts." *The Beehive* (blog), January 16, 2013. Massachusetts Historical Society. https://www.masshist.org.

Glenn, Joshua. "Looking for Mr. Boston." *Boston Globe*, December 28, 2003.

Maggiolo, Chris. *Distilled in Vermont: A History & Guide with Cocktail Recipes.* Charleston, SC: The History Press, 2020.

Morson, Jenn. "Cheers! Nantucket's Triple Eight Distillery." *The Take Magazine*, October 28, 2017. https://thetakemagazine.com.

Pogash, Jonathan, Rick Rodgers, and Ben Fink. *Mr. Boston Official Bartender's Guide: 75th Anniversary Edition*. Hoboken, NJ: John Wiley & Sons, 2012.

Regan, Gary, and Mardee Haidin Regan. *The Book of Bourbon and Other Fine American Whiskeys*. Boston, MA: Houghton Mifflin, 1995.

Risen, Clay. "Back in the Mix: New England Rum." *New York Times*, October 30, 2012.

Seaburg, Carl, and Alan Seaburg. *Medford on the Mystic*. Medford, MA: Medford Historical Society, 1980.

Valaer, Peter. "Foreign and Domestic Rum." *Industrial and Engineering Chemistry* 29, no. 9 (September 1, 1937).

Washburne, George R., and Stanley Bronner (eds.) *Beverages De Luxe*. Louisville, KY: Bulletin Publishing, 1914.

Wilbur, C. Keith. *Picture Book of the Revolution's Privateers*. Harrisburg, PA: Stackpole Books, 1973.

Additional Resources

Websites of the distilleries were consulted.

Personal interviews were conducted with distillery owners, distillers and other related individuals.

ABOUT THE AUTHOR

Zachary Lamothe is the author of four other books, including *Connecticut Lore: Strange, Off-Kilter and Full of Surprises*, *More Connecticut Lore: Guidebook to 82 Strange Locations*, *A History Lover's Guide to the South Shore* and *Classic Restaurants of Boston*. He graduated from Boston University with a degree in American Studies and holds a master's degree from Southern Connecticut State University in education. He also runs the website Backyard Road Trips and cohosts the *Backyard Road Trips* podcast. He lives in Plymouth, Massachusetts, with his wife, Jaclyn, three sons, one dog and one cat.

Visit us at
www.historypress.com
....